SACRED DRIVE

SACRED DRIVE

BIBLICAL PRINCIPLES FOR PURSUING YOUR GOD-GIVEN POTENTIAL

VAUGHN KOHLER

ISBN 13: 978-1-63489-425-8

Library of Congress Catalog Number has been applied for.
Printed in the United States of America
First Printing: 2021

25   24 23 22 21   5   4   3   2   1

Cover design by Luke Bird
Interior design by Patrick Maloney

Wise Ink Creative Publishing
807 Broadway St NE
Suite 46
Minneapolis, MN, 55413

This book is dedicated to my wife, Kasia,
and my daughters, Lila, Veronica, Mariah, and Emma Jane.
I want to pursue my potential, not just for the glory
of God and good of the world,
but to be what you deserve: the best possible husband and father.
Kocham cię bardzo!

CONTENTS

Acknowledgments   ix

Introduction   1

1. Put In More   11

2. Hard -> Happy   17

3. Expect a Battle   23

4. Win the Day   29

5. Seek to See   35

6. Take It "Bird by Bird"   41

7. Follow the Pattern   47

8. Embrace Motivating Grace   55

9. Play Your Note   65

10. Confess to Crush   73

11. Say "Yes, Sir"   85

12. Accept Gifts, Eliminate Idols   95

13. Do You (AMDG)   109

14. Value Your Body   117

15. Pursue Lifelong Learning   125

16. Let Pain Empower You   135

17. Give God Now   143

Conclusion   151

About the Author   159

ACKNOWLEDGMENTS

I'd like to start by thanking my wife, my daughters, my mom, my brothers, my sisters-in-law, and all the members of our family, just for being the gifts of God that you are. Thanks for contributing to the stories in this book. I love you!

To my many great friends: there are too many to name, you know who you are. I love you all!

(That said, a special word of appreciation to Chris and Liane Saunders and Dr. Alex Spinoso, for *specifically* encouraging me to pursue my God-given potential and write a book! There have been many others who nudged me to write a book, but you were the loudest, sexiest voices)

Of course, I'm incredibly grateful for everyone at 1st Phorm who has been used by God to help me get more out of myself and my life: Andy Frisella, Sal Frisella, Jim Frisella, Emily Frisella, Chris Klein, Jason Caine, Drew Skyles, Jarrett Bond . . . I know I'm forgetting amazing people. I do wish I could list you all by name! You have definitely taught me to "never settle."

Thanks to Ed Mylett, Josh Levin, and Ben Newman (EMAW! Pound the Stone!) for being three outstanding examples in my life of men of faith who are also driven to succeed at everything they do.

Thanks to the students in the Grace Baptist youth group (hey GYM!) from 2002 to 2011. It was such an honor and privilege to serve you. You helped me grow in faith, hope, and love; and "I thank God every time I remember you" (Philippians 1:3).

In addition, I am so grateful for Amy, Graham, Luke, and the exceptional team at Wise Ink Creative Publishing. This book would not have come into existence without your expert feedback and guidance!

And, of course, I can't help but express my deepest gratitude to my patron saint, Saint Philip Neri, and, far more than anyone else, to the Prince of Peace and King of Kings.

When my spirit clothed immortal
Wings its flight through the realms of the day
This my song through endless ages
Jesus led me all the way

INTRODUCTION

"Do not be afraid. Do not be satisfied with mediocrity. Put out into the deep and let out your nets for
a catch." —**Pope Saint John Paul the Great**

"The world has yet to see what God can do [with some-
one] who is fully consecrated to him." —**D. L. Moody**

"Let's roll!" —**Optimus Prime**

We live in a success-driven culture. A lot of people want to pursue their full potential, to get more out of themselves and their lives. Are you one of them?

We also live in a culture full of people who, in spite of declining numbers in church attendance, still consider themselves "spiritual." Are you one of them?

In the last several years, I've lived at the crossroads between spirituality and "success." I transitioned from full-time ministry to working in the world of entrepreneurship and self-development, what is sometimes referred to as the "success and motivation" space.

(Don't feel bad if you are suspicious of that space. I was—and still am. I'll get to that.)

From 2002 to 2011, I was an associate pastor at Grace Baptist Church in Manhattan, Kansas, working primarily with students from middle school to college. (Go K-State!) Those were good years. I consider myself extremely privileged to have been called to minister to that congregation, especially the kids in the youth group, who treated their pastor far better than I deserved. Whatever fruits of Christian maturity can be found in their lives today are ultimately the result of God's grace and their parents' faithfulness, but it was an enormous blessing to play even the smallest part in encouraging them to grow in faith, hope, and love.

In 2011, I left the ministry for two reasons. The first was that, after much study and prayer, I decided to seek full communion in the Catholic Church. (That's a whole 'nother story, but if you want to learn more about it, go to YouTube and search "Vaughn Kohler: The Journey Home.") The second was that, because of my love of writing, speaking, and college students, I wanted to pursue a career as a professor of communications.

My pursuit of that goal did not work out. In fact, for about a year after my family and I moved from Kansas to St. Louis, I bounced around from one job to the next. In the space of about fourteen months, I served as marketing director for an architectural metals company named Parasoleil, trained to be a salesman for Tri-County Water & Air, started my own business as a ghostwriter, and even did a stint as a writer and editor for a startup magazine that wanted to be a kind of *GQ* or *Esquire* for St. Louis (except that their mission was to "make men better men").

As God's providence would have it, while I wasn't on the path I'd had in mind for myself, he was guiding me down an entirely different road—one that would take me places I couldn't have imagined.

During my tenure at the magazine, I was asked to write an article on a local entrepreneur named Andy Frisella. Andy and his partner, Chris Klein, had taken the money they earned from painting stripes on parking lots, started a nutritional supplement business, and built it into a nine-figure empire. (The name of their retail company is Supplement Superstores, and the name of the company that produces the actual supplements is 1st Phorm.)

Andy is a very big, bearded, muscle-bound Italian with an iron gaze and an intimidating presence. He knows how to string together F-bombs in rapid succession and cuss like it's an art form. As his Instagram bio states, he is "not for everyone"—and if you are someone who can't learn powerful lessons about business and life from a man who uses salty language, he's definitely not for you.

But he's definitely for me—because his friendship and influence on my life are how this book came to be written in the first place.

When I interviewed Andy, the two of us hit it off. (We talked about our mutual love of dogs for the first half hour.) After the article was published, I delivered a copy of the magazine to him and mentioned that, with all his experience and expertise, he should write a book.

"I should," he said. "And I am a good writer. But I don't have the time."

I suggested that I help him write it. He agreed, we started working together—and that's when something really amazing happened.

Andy's team recorded us as I interviewed him multiple times, on topics ranging from marketing to mental toughness. They started posting clips of his answers on social media . . .

. . . and people went crazy.

Remember when I said I wasn't totally comfortable with the "success and motivation" space? Neither is Andy. We both believe it's full of cheesy gurus, life coaches with no real authority to tell anyone how to live, and shallow, superficial scam artists out to inflate people's egos and make a quick buck.

I believe the reason people went crazy when they saw those clips of Andy—the reason people love him in general—is his unique, no-nonsense, punch-you-in-the-face-with-the-truth style. They recognize that, in a world full of faux entrepreneurs and internet scammers, Andy is the real deal. He actually built a business from the ground up, and the principles of success and excellence that he championed produced real results in his own business and life.

So people started asking, "Are these clips from your podcast? Where can I find your podcast?"

To make a long story short, Andy didn't even know what a podcast was, but he decided that what he had to share could genuinely help people—personally and professionally. He decided to start a podcast called *The MFCEO Project* (yes, that stands for what you think it stands for) and asked me to be the cohost! A fire-breathing, F-bomb-dropping entrepreneur and a former pastor talking about business and success? Turns out it was a winning combination. Barely a couple months into the debut on iTunes, *The MFCEO Project* was earning millions of downloads a month and was consistently ranked among the top ten podcasts in the world.

Serving as Andy's podcast cohost snowballed into working for him full time, and that's when my life really changed forever. Although I was primarily helping him to develop his personal brand, I also started working at 1st Phorm headquarters and officially became a part of the company culture. On a day-to-day basis, Andy pushed me to do my absolute best and to be more committed to excellence, productivity, and hard work. On a weekly basis, I listened to him and his brother Sal give company talks about becoming detail oriented, going the extra mile, and being a problem solver. I have never been in a more challenging environment, and while it wasn't fun at times (Andy has no problem letting you know—very directly—when you are giving anything less than your best effort), my standards were steadily rising. I was developing traits that I'd previously lacked—traits like discipline, directness, and follow-through. Instead of just relying on the natural talent and intelligence God had given me, I started putting in much harder work to get more out of myself and do more with the life I'd been given.

The reality is, the longer I was around Andy and worked with him, the more I realized that (1) the principles of excellence and success he lived by actually helped me become a stronger Christian, and (2) the reason for this is that most of the principles themselves can be found in the Bible!

I've known my whole life that the Bible talks a lot about worship, prayer, giving to the poor, and loving your enemy. But it wasn't until I met such a driven man and was immersed in a culture that was so aggressively committed to excellence—and yes, to *winning*—that I went back to the Bible and discovered that it has a ton to say about so many of the topics that are associated with self-development and the "success and motivation" space. In fact, while Andy was my catalyst in seeking success, I realized that I'd already been learning lessons in that area—the lessons that had been teaching me how to be a better Christian.

As you will see in this book, the Bible has much to say about things like vision, discipline, self-mastery, mental toughness, time management, and perseverance. There is no question in my mind that God wants us to pursue a successful life here on earth—but we have to let his Word define exactly what that means. There is also no doubt in my mind that God wants us to pursue the potential that he himself gave us. If we strive to become all that he intended us to be, that will result in his glory. If we marshal all our strength to do everything he has called us to do, that will result in good for the world. Introducing Andy into my life is only the biggest of many nudges God has given me toward reaching the goals he has in mind for me—time and again he's placed me in situations that would push me toward glorifying him and bettering myself and others.

From the very first episode of *The MFCEO Project* in June 2015, Andy gave me the nickname "the Pastor of Disaster." People who listen to the show know I used to be in full-time ministry, and for that reason, I have gotten all sorts of questions on different spiritual topics. I've also been honored that people have asked me to pray for them and give them some counsel on tough situations they have faced in life.

One question in particular has been asked time and time again by fellow Christians: "Is it okay for me to be ambitious?" In other words, is it okay for a Christian to want to be financially successful, to be in the best possible physical shape, to crush lofty goals, or to exercise great influence in the world? In many cases, these are fellow Christians who want to be, say, a dominating head football coach, the top salesperson in their company, a Fortune 500 entrepreneur, or a worldwide social media influencer.

Should they feel guilty about that?

My answer to them—and to you? There is sinful ambition, and there is holy ambition. We can be driven to excellence and success by our selfish ego, simply wanting to make a name for ourselves and amass material possessions for their own sake. Or we can work to cultivate what I'd like to call *sacred drive*—a righteous motivation to pursue our God-given potential, not just for our gain, but for God's glory and the good of the world.

This book is my humble attempt to help you do that. It is by no means an exhaustive treatment of every conceivable Biblical principle that might help us motivate ourselves to pursue our God-given potential, but it does cover the fundamentals. If, in the future, I come to the conviction that additional topics need to be added to the book . . . I'll just publish a revised and expanded edition!

Although I'm writing from a distinctly Christian perspective and the chapters you are about to read unpack ancient truths found in the Bible, I believe this book will be helpful for any open-minded person who is success oriented and spiritually minded. But it's specifically intended for followers of Jesus Christ—of any tradition or denomination—who want to pursue their God-given potential. It is for those who don't want to live with a sense of frustration or failure, but to experience growth, satisfaction, enthusiasm, and the peace of mind that they have given, as Oswald Chambers once put it, "my utmost for His Highest."

None of us who follow the Savior want to squander the talents and opportunities that God has given us. None of us want to come to the end of the day—or the end of our lives!—and think, *My God, I've wasted it.* No. We want to live with all our might and to work at everything as "unto the Lord." We want to be faithful stewards of every day that God has put us on this earth (Colossians 3:23) so that someday we will hear, "Well done, my good and faithful servant. Enter now into the joy of your master" (Matthew 25:23).

To be clear, this book isn't about becoming a better Christian *per se.* It is about becoming a Christian who knows why and how to become better, at whatever it is we choose to do—whether that is sharing the gospel, getting in shape, or scaling a business to nine figures. I absolutely want you to use the principles found in this book for your own gain, but not your gain alone. I want you to pursue your full potential for your gain, the good of the world, and the glory of God! You don't have to choose just one motivation. You can be guided by all three.

As Andy has told me again and again, the pursuit of our potential is exactly that—a pursuit. We will never actually achieve perfection until we're in heaven with Jesus, Mary, my dog Rudy, and all the saints. Personally, I'm nowhere close to where I want to be in terms of fulfilling the potential God gave me. But I'm further along than I was last year, and I'm light years ahead of where I was a decade ago. Even if I sputter, stall, or have a setback, one thing's for sure: I'm never going to give up. No matter how much frustration and failure I experience, I will press on, for I am determined to never abandon my calling to make much of Jesus and make the most of my life. God has given me life and given me potential, and it's just plain wrong for me to not go all in for the Almighty—in every area of my life.

Do you feel the same way?

Okay, then . . .

. . . LET'S ROLL!

Vaughn Kohler
Manhattan, Kansas

Chapter One

PUT IN MORE

"Pray as though everything depended on God. Work as though everything depended on you." **—Saint Augustine**

"The formula for misery = huge dreams + crap work ethic." **—Ed Mylett**

In the summer of 2006, I took a group of kids on a mission trip to inner-city Chicago, along with a group led by my friend Trent. We were there to serve the poor and homeless and do some street preaching.

By that time, I had already earned my master of divinity degree, which included 120 credit hours of biblical studies, philosophy, church history, Hebrew, Greek, and other related subjects. At the risk of sounding arrogant, I hadn't found the program extremely challenging. That's not to say I always got straight As, but with a little extra effort, I could have. Oftentimes, even when I barely studied, I earned a B or a B plus in classes as difficult as "Greek Exegesis of Paul's Letter to the Romans."

For the longest time, I thought of myself as an amazingly intelligent guy. I was able to neglect my studies in favor of watching sports, hanging out with my friends, and generally goofing around—and still earn Bs, even As! On top of that, God had gifted me with a good memory, so much of what I *did* study, I retained. I wore my ability to get results while essentially coasting through the program as a badge of honor.

However, on this mission trip, I encountered a young man who completely rocked my view of myself.

This kid was from Trent's youth group. The first time I saw him, he was sitting in the corner of the big meeting room we were all gathered in, and he was holding a Bible about two inches from his face—so close, it was like he was about to put it on and wear it as a mask. On top of that, he was turning his head back and forth across the pages, muttering to himself under his breath.

Either he was a weirdo who was just goofing off for attention, I thought, or he was a lunatic.

"What on earth is he doing?" I asked Trent.

Trent smiled. "James has two strikes against him," he said. "He has a learning disability and a vision problem that makes it exceedingly difficult to read."

Hearing that, I felt like a total donkey. I had judged this young man without taking the time to understand him and the situation. "That's rough," I said.

"Oh, don't feel bad for James," replied Trent. "He's determined and relentless. Nobody in our youth group knows the Bible better than he does."

As the impact of that statement slammed into me, I thought of Jesus's words: "To whom much is given, much is required." God had given me a lot of intellectual gifts, but I had neglected them. He had given virtually nothing to James, but James had maximized what he had. There was no question in my mind who had been more faithful to God's blessings on his life.

Of the many stories in the Gospels, the one that I feel is profoundly relevant to pursuing our God-given potential is the story of the widow's offering in Luke 21:1–4. In this story, Jesus is at the temple as all the wealthy people are putting their gifts into the offering. When they are finished, a poor widow approaches and contributes "two small copper coins" (the sources I consulted said that, in today's economy, that's only two dollars!) In response, Jesus says, "Truly, I tell you, this poor widow has put in more than all of them. For they all contributed out of their abundance, but she out of her poverty put in all she had to live on."

Jesus wasn't impressed by the wealthy folks in this scenario because their giving didn't require much sacrifice. That's what he meant by "they gave out of their abundance." In other words, it was no skin off their back to part with several hundred dollars—because they had several thousand in the bank! Who knows? They could have just been donating the interest they made off the whopping sum in their account. (I don't even know if they had banks or interest back then, but hopefully, you get my point!)

In contrast, the widow really put herself out there. According to Jesus, she was a woman of "poverty," and yet she took what little she had and went all in with it. From Jesus' perspective, she *put in more* than all the rich people combined.

The point is that it isn't how much you have that honors God. It's your willingness to go all in with what you do have— even to the point of real sacrifice.

From our limited, earthly perspective, a daughter born into a wealthy family has an advantage over a son born to a single mother in poverty. From a spiritual perspective, she doesn't. Both are held to the same standard: *make the most of what you have.* If that young man works hard and rises above his socioeconomic status while the young woman underachieves in her inherited role of CEO, he is the one who is more faithful to what God has given him.

In the same way, the third-stringer who plays his heart out is superior to the All-American athlete who has great stats but underachieves compared to his full potential. The mildly talented piano student whose fingers bleed from practicing so hard is superior to the musical prodigy who half-asses the cultivation of his gift. The man who inherits a position as CEO of a billion-dollar company and takes it for granted is inferior to a young girl with special needs who sets up a lemonade stand and puts her whole heart into selling Dixie Cups full of her sweet drink to the whole neighborhood.

Ecclesiastes 9:10 says, "Whatever your hand finds to do, work at it *with all your might.*" Colossians 3:23 says, "Whatever you do, *work as unto the Lord,* not men, for it is the Lord you are serving." And when the disciple Peter asked Jesus what his plan was for the disciple John, Jesus replied, "What is that to you? *You* follow me" (emphasis mine).

The work of our lives is not measured by how it compares to others'. As Andy Frisella says, "*You* are the measure of your success. It's not how much you have accomplished. It's how much you *could have* accomplished. Success is the pursuit of *your own* full potential."

That statement is 100 percent consistent with what the Scriptures teach. We are not responsible for eclipsing the achievements of others. We are called to relentlessly strive to become all God has made us to be, and to maximize every resource he has given us—from the money in our bank account to whatever artistic talent we possess.

Therefore, the driving question behind our desire to pursue our potential should be, "What can I do to *take what God has given me . . . and put in more*?"

Put in more effort to develop the talents he's given me.

Put in more time to serve the people around me.

Put in more of my resources to support his work in the world.

Put more of myself into everything I do . . .

. . . so that I become all that he wants me to be.

What should ultimately motivate us to become focused, confident, disciplined, and determined is not a desire to one-up others or win more than anyone else (or to put more money in the offering plate). It should be a desire for our one life to always move upward as we relentlessly work to get more out of ourselves and give back more of what God has given us—whether that's our time, talent, or treasure.

For spiritually minded people who want to pursue their God-given potential, that's what it all comes down to.

God has put so much potential in our lives. Our job is to put *so much more* into the life he has given us.

QUESTIONS FOR REFLECTION

• How would you evaluate your effort to make the most of what God has given you in the following areas of your life: talents, time, resources, and opportunities?

- What specific talent will you choose to relentlessly cultivate for your gain, the good of the world, and the glory of God?

RECOMMENDED RESOURCES

- *Don't Waste Your Life* by John Piper

- *The Treasure Principle: Unlocking the Secret of Joyful Giving* by Randy Alcorn

- *#MAXOUT Your Life: Strategies for Becoming an Elite Performer* by Ed Mylett

Chapter Two

HARD → HAPPY

"All men seek happiness. This is without exception. Whatever different means they employ, they all tend to this end. The cause of some going to war, and of others avoiding it, is the same desire in both, attended with different views. The will never takes the least step but to this object. This is the motive of every action of every man, even of those who hang themselves." —**Blaise Pascal**

"Let us run with perseverance the race marked out for us, fixing our eyes on Jesus, the pioneer and perfecter of faith. For the joy set before him he endured the cross, scorning its shame, and sat down at the right hand of the throne of God." —**Hebrews 12:1b-2**

"Then Jesus told his disciples, 'If anyone would come after me, let him deny himself and take up his cross and follow me. For whoever would save his life will lose it, but whoever loses his life for my sake will find it.'" —**Matthew 16:24-25**

I am the least handy man alive. Manual skills waved me bye-bye a long time ago.

When my dad was alive, he could fix anything around the house. My older brother inherited that trait. So, over the years, depending on where I lived, when something needed fixing or improving, I asked my family for help, or my father-in-law, John (who is a contractor), or my old neighbors John Harrington or Chuck Zadow, who are both from that generation that seems to know how to do anything. (John once helped us capture a snake that had gotten loose in our basement, and Chuck was always my go-to guy for landscaping advice.)

On one very unique occasion, however, I decided to try my hand at a major task: installing a new garbage disposal.

I can't stress to you how far outside my comfort zone—and natural talents—this was. It involved wiring (splicing a connection to a new power cord), plumbing (cutting PVC pipe, using plumber's putty to seal things up), and carefully reading a twenty-seven-step instruction manual, which, for me, was like reading a Russian grammar textbook written in Polish.

My father-in-law (remember, the contractor) says that installing a new garbage disposal is actually kind of tricky.

For me, it was hard. Very hard. I almost quit when I couldn't figure out how to hold the flange in place and put on the snap ring. It took me forever. There was a real chance of cataclysmic failure.

But I finished it. It looked beautiful. And—most importantly—it worked!

I know this sounds crazy, but something really extraordinary happened when I stood there in front of the sink and said to myself, "I did it. I did that."

I got emotional.

I experienced a wave of feelings: gratitude, satisfaction, pride, excitement.

I did something that, for me, was very hard . . .

. . . and it produced happiness!

The really amazing thing is that it produced more happiness than I had experienced . . .

. . . watching *The Office* (my favorite show)

. . . or eating a bowl of Daiquiri Ice from Baskin-Robbins (my favorite ice cream)

. . . or pulling out of the car dealership with my sweet new Honda Accord with leather interior ("If you have the means, I highly recommend picking one up").

What I experienced in the situation with the garbage disposal actually illustrates a truth that is found in Scripture and is a plain fact of the universe, but it's not one that everyone readily acknowledges.

Here's what I'm talking about:

Everyone wants to be happy, but very few people actually know—or better yet, are willing to accept—the true path to happiness. In the mind of the average person, happiness comes with things that make life easier and more pleasurable: a surplus of money in the bank, a multimillion dollar home in Palm Beach, a Rolls or Lambo in the driveway, and the resources to escape reality at any time by flying private to Bora Bora or the Swiss Alps. You know, the simple pleasures.

None of these things is intrinsically immoral—enjoying them as gifts of God can be holy, right, and good. However, if you look to these things for your ultimate happiness, they cease to be gifts and become what the Bible calls idols: false gods. Created things that take the place of the one, true Creator. This is not only misguided and wrong; it is the very essence of sin.

When we center our hope for happiness on idols that promise ease and comfort, the result is anything but true happiness. Easy living leads to spiritual dullness and complacency.

Comfort leads to flakiness and entitlement. The pursuit of nothing but easy pleasure ironically leads to the inability to experience peace or genuine enjoyment. (I'll talk about idolatry again a little later in this book.)

There is no question that God wants us to be happy. But he wants us to find our happiness in what he knows will provide the only true, deep, and lasting satisfaction: himself!

"Delight yourself in the Lord, and he will give you the desires of your heart" (Psalm 37:4).

"Be glad in the Lord" (Psalm 32:11).

"Rejoice in the Lord!" (Philippians 3:1).

"Do your acts with cheerfulness" (Romans 12:8).

"Serve the Lord with gladness" (Psalm 100:2).

But here's the key: we achieve that happiness in him—and by extension, true happiness in life—not by pursuing ease and comfort but by willingly choosing the hard path. In fact, he calls us to embrace things that, apart from his grace, are not only difficult but impossible.

We are to stop making excuses, humble ourselves, and admit that we are powerless to save ourselves. We are to be radical in our battle against our own weaknesses and sins. We are to be willing to sacrifice our own desires for the glory of God and the good of others. We are to work for peace and justice. We are to stand for the truth when the crowd delights in lies. Above all, we are to do everything in our power to be good stewards of the life God has given us—making the best use of our time, managing our money well, and making the most of our talents.

Jesus promised us happiness: "I have come that you may

have and enjoy life, and have it abundantly" (John 10:10). But he was also very clear how that would happen: "If anyone would come after me, let him deny himself and take up his cross and follow me. For whoever would save his life will lose it, but whoever loses his life for my sake will find it" (Matthew 16:24–15).

Jesus rose from the dead and ascended into heaven. But only after he hung on a Roman cross—an instrument of excruciating suffering and death. We can have happiness in life. But only by our willingness to do that which is hard.

So in practical terms, that means that pursuing our God-given potential is not going to be easy. As our minds are transformed by God's spirit and the truth, we must strive to become people of focus, determination, and grit. Saint Paul put it this way: "*discipline yourself* for the purpose of godliness" (1 Timothy 4:7b, emphasis mine).

Developing discipline is never easy! But that God-empowered discipline is what will drive the growth of our holiness, our love, and our ability to influence and impact the world. When we commit to doing the hard work of embracing God's calling on our lives, the results are life-changing—for ourselves and everyone on earth.

So much is offered to us. But there can be no happiness apart from taking the hard path, no delight without discipline, and no significant impact on the world without self-mastery.

The soul cannot grow without grace-infused mental toughness—which I would define as the willingness and ability to do hard things and to choose the hard path. But when we start cultivating it, mental toughness is grace of God for the soul!

In order to successfully pursue your God-given potential, get used to doing hard things. Commit to doing hard things. Fully understand and embrace the truth that there is a hard path to happiness. Dedicate yourself to the painstaking work of cultivating mental toughness. Discover for yourself the spiritual, physical, and practical benefits of focus, discipline, grit, and perseverance.

Always remember: hard leads to happy!

QUESTIONS FOR REFLECTION

• How has your lack of mental toughness (the willingness and ability to do hard things and choose the hard path) influenced your experience of happiness?

• How could you make more of an impact for Christ in the world if you were disciplined in the pursuit of your God-given potential?

RECOMMENDED RESOURCES

• *Celebration of Discipline: The Path to Spiritual Growth* by Richard Foster

• *Resisting Happiness* by Matthew Kelly

• *75Hard: A Tactical Guide to Winning the War with Yourself* by Andy Frisella (warning: explicit language)

Chapter Three

EXPECT A BATTLE

"In the early days, when Christianity exercised a dominant influence over American thinking, men conceived the world to be a battleground. Our fathers believed in sin and the devil and hell as constituting one force, and they believed in God and righteousness and heaven as the other. By their very nature, these forces were opposed to each other forever in deep, grave, irreconcilable hostility. Man, our fathers held, had to choose sides—he could not be neutral. For him it must be life or death, heaven or hell, and if he chooses to come out on God's side, he could expect open war with God's enemies. The fight would be real and deadly and would last as long as life continued here below. Men looked forward to heaven as a return from the wars, a laying down of the sword to enjoy in peace the home prepared for them." **—A.W. Tozer**

"This is a dojo, not a knitting class!"
—John Kreese, Cobra Kai sensei

I am shameless in my belief that *The Karate Kid* (1984) is the greatest movie ever made.

I know every frame in that movie backward and forward, and I could probably quote the entire script with very few prompts.

If you are unfamiliar with the film, I feel very sorry for you—because you haven't lived if you've never seen the most inspirational piece of cinema ever made.

"Finish him!"

"Get him a body bag! Yeah!"

"Daniel! You did it! You did it!"

If you don't know what I'm talking about, find out. Your life will never be the same.

The basic premise of the movie: loveable loser Daniel LaRusso moves from Newark, New Jersey, to Los Angeles, California, where he is regularly bullied and beaten up by a gang of cool kids trained in karate. At a critical point in the movie, Daniel is befriended by an Okinawan handyman named Mr. Miyagi, who is himself a master of martial arts.

Eventually, Mr. Miyagi trains Daniel in karate, but initially, he simply accompanies Daniel to the Cobra Kai karate school, where all the psychopathic cool kids are being taught by the villainous sensei, John Kreese. Miyagi asks Kreese to tell his students to leave Daniel alone.

"What's the matter?" Kreese asks. "The boy can't take care of himself?"

Miyagi begins to explain the situation, but Kreese blows up.

"This is a karate dojo, not a knitting class!"

Kreese is a bad dude and not much can be said about his character. As the founder of the dojo and the sensei of Cobra Kai, he wields tremendous influence—influence he could have used to keep Daniel from getting bullied. But he doesn't. So, in that particular scenario, he is clearly in the wrong.

From a broader perspective, though, he is correct. Applied to the nature of the universe, his sentiment—whether we like it or not—is true. Life is full of conflict—conflict that we have to train hard to handle.

It's a fact. The world is a dojo, not a knitting class.

Not enough people understand this.

Too many people lack the ability to grow in faith and maximize their God-given potential because they have a view of the world that is both naive and at odds with what the Scriptures teach. All concrete evidence and divine revelation unanimously declares that the world is a battleground, not a playground, but their warped thinking persists.

It's astonishing how many people believe the world owes them happiness simply because they exist. When they discover that no one is entitled to a life without disadvantage, difficulty, or disappointment, it's a hard blow. Even though for centuries scientists have described the world as a competition in which species find their niche or die, these misguided people think all that is required to prosper in life is to participate. They believe that feeling good about yourself is an automatic fact of life, and that never—under any circumstances—should anyone keep score in sports, business, or society. They don't understand that confidence and a clear conscience have to be earned, and when others win they want to know why everyone can't. Nature demands that they work hard and compete to be victorious, but too often they embrace the mentality of a victim.

Interestingly enough, the same misguided mentality is found in many of those who claim to have a relationship with Jesus. When they first entrust their lives to Christ, they somehow believe that they have been given leave to desert the battlefield and return to the Garden of Eden. They don't seem to understand that thousands of years ago, a snake entered the garden and the first humans were expelled. Since that time, the whole universe has been at war.

Today in America, after a person is baptized, we hold a party, take photos, and post about it on Facebook to see how many likes we'll get. In the early days of the Church, a person who professed faith and was baptized was often given a swift smack in the face by a bishop. It was a symbolic gesture, meant to say, "Time to toughen up. This is going to be rough. Prepare for battle!"

For most of the history of Christianity, believers understood that following Christ means that you suddenly have three enemies: Satan, who prowls around wanting to destroy your soul; your own sinfulness, which weighs on you and drags you downward; and the world at large, which wants you to be driven by greed instead of godliness, pride instead of purity, and selfishness instead of justice.

Most of us today simply do not understand that growing in faith, hope, and love is a battle. We don't fully comprehend that the pursuit of our God-given potential is not a carefree stroll down Main Street in Branson, Missouri. It's more like landing on the beaches of Normandy!

For this reason, believers are easily disappointed and disillusioned. They lose faith and fall to temptation because their expectations of life with God were totally wrong. They fell for the lie of the worst hymn ever written: "Every day with Jesus is sweeter than the day before."

Some days are going to be savage—and sting. Of course, that doesn't mean Jesus himself isn't sweet and satisfying, or that his grace is somehow deficient. But it does mean that there will be days when you are in Satan's crosshairs, when you are war-weary from your own flaws and failures, when you feel distant from God, dry in your spiritual life, and driven to the point of frustration, fear, and faithlessness. There are going to be days when your family is at odds with each other, your friends are off doing their own thing, your finances are in disarray, and the forces of your country and culture seem like they are doing everything possible to drive you out of your mind.

On those days, you have to remind yourself that you are at war. You have to, as Saint Paul says, "put on the full armor of God to take your stand against the devil and his schemes." You have to understand that your mission in life isn't ultimately to achieve your American dream, but to "please your commanding officer." You have to look to the saints and angels as your indispensable allies in the fight of life and faith, and you have to do everything you can to win the battle: Be sober-minded and alert (1 Peter 5:8). Make no provision for the flesh (Romans 13:14). Be well-armed: wage war with prayer, the Sword of the Spirit, the Word of God. (Ephesians 6). You have to take the Bible seriously when it says that, while it is Christ who upholds us with his grace and power (Hebrews 1:3), it is nevertheless true that "only those who endure to the end will be saved" (Matthew 24:13). You must conduct yourself like a "good soldier of Christ" (2 Timothy 2:3) so that at the end of your life, you can say "I fought the good fight" (2 Timothy 4:7–8).

Oh, and in case you never saw the greatest movie ever made, wimpy underdog Daniel submitted to the wise instruction of Mr. Miyagi. He endured a grueling training regimen of waxing cars, painting fences, and sanding floors and transformed himself into something of a New Jersey Ninja. (Uh, kind of.) After systematically knocking every slithery thug out of the All-Valley Karate Tournament, he took on Johnny Lawrence, the King Cobra himself—and won.

That's how it's done!

Life is a battleground, not a playground. It's a dojo, not a knitting class. You can't come here to planet Earth, live in this world, ignore the challenges, drop your guard, and expect to be without scars. No, you've got to get your mind right on the true nature of life, or you're going to have a major problem.

QUESTIONS FOR REFLECTION

• What areas of your life are you wrongly expecting to be easy and unchallenging?

• How can being more realistic about the battleground nature of life and faith help you experience more success?

RECOMMENDED RESOURCES

• *Prayers against the Powers of Darkness* published by the United States Conference of Catholic Bishops

• *Angels: God's Secret Agents* by Billy Graham

• Saint Paul's Letter to the Ephesians (especially chapter 6), Holy Bible

• *Can't Hurt Me: Master Your Mind and Defy the Odds* by David Goggins

Chapter Four

WIN THE DAY

"Do not worry about tomorrow; let tomorrow worry about itself. Each day has trouble of its own." **—Jesus**

"The life of faith is lived one day at a time, and it has to be lived—not always looked forward to as though the 'real' living were around the next corner. It is today for which we are responsible. God still owns tomorrow."**—Elisabeth Elliot**

Too many people are petrified and paralyzed because they want to tackle the grand plan for their life . . . right now. They want to know the detailed blueprint for their entire destiny . . . right away.

Well, in St. Louis, where I used to live, there's a huge church called the Cathedral Basilica of Saint Louis. If you were to enter the cathedral and look up at the ceiling, you would see beautiful depictions of grand, epic scenes from the Bible. But if you were to look closer, you'd see these stunning works of art are actually composed of these tiny ceramic squares—which are usually one color.

The way to create this masterpiece is to affix one square to the ceiling, then another square, and another, and another, and so on . . . and over time, the image begins to form. The final result is hundreds of fragments made into a beautiful whole.

These mosaics don't just honor God through their

beauty—the way they're made represents a fundamental principle of the mental toughness he desires of us. That old saying, "Yard by yard, life is hard; inch by inch, it's a cinch," is based on a spiritual truth in the Bible: we are to focus on one day at a time, even one moment at a time.

We're never going to be able to pursue our potential and create the work of art that our life is meant to be all at once. Instead, we need to ask ourselves, "What's the block of color I need to put on the ceiling today? Where's the next little square go? What color does it need to be?" Over time, if you focus on block after block and square after square, the image is going to take shape . . . your understanding of what you need to do is going to fully form. Once it has, you'll be able to step back, take in the whole picture at once, and say, "Wow, hard to imagine that I created such a masterpiece."

You created it . . . because you took one piece at a time. You lived one day at a time. You did the next right thing.

Here's the bottom line: uncertainty causes anxiety. Attempting too much at once causes us to be overwhelmed.

You need to work to win the day. Don't let uncertainty keep you from being intentional. You don't need *the* plan for your *whole life* right now. You just need *a* plan for *your life right now*. You need to focus on winning the twenty-four hours that you have in front of you.

This is not just a practical approach to success and productivity in life. It is a philosophy rooted in and founded upon Scriptural truth.

In the Sermon on the Mount, Jesus preached to people whose cares and concerns dwarfed our own. Israel existed under occupation by the Roman Empire, similar to how the Austrians existed under German control during World War II or the Poles were ruled by the Soviet Union after the war. Although the Romans were fairly lenient as occupying powers go, when they said "jump," the Jewish people had to ask "how high?" As if that weren't stressful enough, most people in biblical times—definitely the ones Jesus preached to—were poor. They barely had clothes on their back, a shelter to live in, or food to eat.

In response to this, Jesus called them to exercise a faith that focused on one day at a time. First, he said, "Why do you worry? Who by worrying can add one day to his life? Consider the lilies of the field: they do not labor or spin, yet the Lord clothes them. Even Solomon in all his splendor was not clothed like one of them. And you are worth more than lilies!" He also said, "Look at the birds of the field; they do not toil or labor, yet your heavenly father feeds them. And you are worth more than many sparrows" (Matthew 6:25–33).

Interestingly enough, Jesus zeroes in on two of the main things humans derive security from: our attractiveness and our productiveness. If we are attractive, society tells us, people will like us and want to help take care of us. If we are productive, we will establish our security in what we produce. In response to this, Jesus points out that lilies, while breathtakingly beautiful, aren't really responsible for their own beauty. Ravens aren't productive at all—they literally do nothing to earn their own keep. Regardless, God takes care of them. Jesus is making a rhetorical point: if I take care of the flowers and birds, who do nothing for themselves, how much more will I take care of you—because you are worth way more than they are to me!

Once we understand this, Jesus says we are to respond this way: "So do not worry about tomorrow; let tomorrow worry about itself. Each day has trouble of its own" (Matthew 6:34). In other words, focus on the twenty-four hours in which you are living. That is the mindset of any believer who wants to pursue—and maximize—their God-given potential. That is the approach to life that leads to success—because it is supported and promoted by Scripture and the Savior himself!

Incidentally, when Jesus taught his disciples to pray, the first request he taught them was, "Give us this day our daily bread." Notice the emphasis on *today*! Jesus tells us to pray, "Right now, God, give me what I need to survive today!" Any Jewish person living in Jesus's time would have automatically noticed a subtle reference to a story from the Old Testament. In the book of Exodus, Israel was wandering in the wilderness. God provided daily bread from heaven that looked like a Keebler sugar wafer and tasted like honey. The people called it "manna," which literally means, "What is it?" It sustained them and kept them alive—but with a catch. God said that you could only gather enough manna for the day. You couldn't keep it overnight. If you did, it would spoil and become inedible. The reason? God wanted to promote a sense of daily dependence on him. He did not want his people worrying about what they were going to eat the next day. All that mattered was the day before them. He would see to the rest.

From the Old Testament to the Sermon on the Mount,

the emphasis is clear: win the day! Focus on the twenty-four hours in which you are living your life.

You want to simultaneously be faithful and focused, to win at life? Win the day. That doesn't mean you should never engage in advanced planning. What it does mean is that your main focus should be the twenty-four hours that are unfolding in front of you. What's the next square you have to put into place?

Saint Paul says, "Be careful, then, how you live, not as unwise, but as wise; making the most of every opportunity, because the days are evil." The Greek word translated as "evil" in context really means "the days are crazy. There's crazy stuff going on." There was then and always has been. For that reason, if you don't want to go insane or be overwhelmed with anxiety but want to be productive and successful in pursuing your potential, focus on making the most of every opportunity *today*. Build the mosaic that is your life one piece at a time.

QUESTIONS FOR REFLECTION

• What method do you have for planning out your day to make sure you make the most of it?

• What are the things that overwhelm you and cause you anxiety that haven't happened yet? How can you prepare for those things in the future while still focusing on what you need to do today?

RECOMMENDED RESOURCES

• *What's Best Next: How the Gospel Transforms the Way You Get Things Done* by Matt Perman

• *The Rhythm of Life: Living Everyday with Passion & Purpose* by Matthew Kelly

Chapter Five

SEEK TO SEE

"Be Thou my Vision, O Lord of my heart
Naught be all else to me, save that Thou art
Thou my best Thought, by day or by night
Waking or sleeping, Thy presence my light"

—Traditional Irish hymn, attributed to Saint Dallán Forgaill

"The most pathetic person in the world is someone
who has sight, but has no vision." **—Helen Keller**

On a cold day in January 2009, I walked into the adoration chapel at St. Agnes Catholic Church in Shawnee, Kansas. At the time, I wasn't Catholic; and if you are reading this and aren't Catholic, you probably don't know right now what I didn't know back then: the purpose of an adoration chapel is to pray and to just *behold* the Blessed Sacrament. That is, it is to gaze at the Eucharist (the wafer used in Communion) and use the "eyes" of your faith to "see" the real presence of Jesus himself.

As my friend Carrie and I knelt down to do just that, I looked over and saw a beautiful woman, probably in her late twenties, kneeling and looking over at us. I didn't know it yet, but she was one of Carrie's roommates. Her eyes were warm and friendly, and she had this big smile on her face, which I

35

interpreted as, *She must think I'm cute.* I found out later that she was actually thinking, *He must not be Catholic. He looks like he has no idea what he's doing!*

Now, as much as I would like to think I have a decent relationship with God, I am definitely no mystic. Yet at that moment, I feel as if something mystical happened. The best way I know how to describe it is by using the words C. S. Lewis used the moment he realized that he believed in Christ: "It was more like when a man, after a long sleep, still lying motionless in bed, becomes aware that *he is now awake.*"

I saw that young woman; and all of a sudden, I felt *awake.* All of a sudden, I felt like my eyes had opened up and I was seeing something I had never seen before. Something new. Something significant.

I didn't know it at that exact moment—though I would know very soon after that—but that was the first time I laid my eyes on the woman who would become my wife.

Seeing her changed the course of my life.

I was uniquely blessed to behold my soul mate at that moment; but in another sense, I was not—and am not—unique at all.

Many, many people have been radically transformed by something they *saw.*

Many, many people have transformed their lives by intentionally beholding what it is they wanted to become, by *seeking to see* what they wanted to experience and achieve.

In every area where human beings seek to become their best and realize their full God-given potential, the top performers *seek to see.* They practice visualization. That is, they form a mental picture (and sometimes use literal pictures) of exactly what it is they want, what they strive for, so that they can meditate on it, imprint it clearly in their minds, and let that vision drive their actions and attitude. The reason they do so is this principle: *what you gaze at is where you go.*

Another way of saying this is that action follows focus. If you know anything about race cars, you might know that rookie drivers make a common mistake. When they see that they're drifting into the outside wall, they panic and start looking at the wall. When this happens, they inevitably end up crashing into it. However, veteran drivers know better. When they sense that they are beginning to drift, they keep their eyes firmly focused on the center of the track. When they do that, their reflexes automatically follow their line of sight. By keeping their gaze on their goal, their whole body gets in line.

The principle of visualization isn't just critical to achieving goals—it's also essential to developing our skills. In his amazingly insightful book *The Talent Code*, Daniel Coyle explains that the most exceptional athletes and performers in every area of life develop their talent by carefully watching the game film of other overachievers in their field. From Olympic-level gymnasts to NFL players, the best of the best spend inordinate amounts of time observing and analyzing the legends of their sport. The late, great Kobe Bryant, for instance, would pore over game films of Michael Jordan. This is just one of the many reasons Kobe became "the next MJ"— but it is a significant reason.

What we who possess a sacred drive need to fully understand is that visualization, or cultivating vision, is an essential practice for pursuing our potential, because it is founded upon an eternal spiritual truth: we are transformed when God *reveals* to us something about himself or the universe that he created. *We are changed by what we see.*

In the Bible, men and women are always radically transformed for the better after they experience a vision of God. Moses was a wandering shepherd until he beheld the glory of God in the burning bush—from that point on, he became God's spokesman to Pharaoh and led the people of Israel out of bondage to Egypt. The prophet Isaiah lived among a wicked people in a corrupt nation. Once he entered the temple and received a powerful vision of God, it changed him completely. He was humbled and motivated to be used however God wanted to use him: "Here I am, Lord. Send me!" (Isaiah 6).

In the New Testament, Saul persecuted and murdered Christians, but after seeing the risen Christ on the road to Damascus, he became a new person altogether. His name became Paul, and he became one of the greatest missionaries, theologians, pastors, and saints of all time (Acts 9). By experiencing a vision of God, we become who God wants us to be—so we ought to intentionally cultivate that vision!

The reality is, the practice of visualization is so much more rich and meaningful for people of faith. Not only can we cultivate our God-given potential and pursue a life of excellence by visualizing our overall dreams and specific goals; not only can we carefully observe the skills that we want to develop in ourselves; but we can also come closer to God by seeking a vision of him through meditating on Scripture, reflecting on the beauty and majesty of nature, and even observing the lives of other faithful believers. "Take note of those who live according to the pattern I gave you," Saint Paul tells his readers in Philippians 3:17. In other words, keep your eyes on the saints!

In the early days of the Church, before the average person could read, it was very common for the people to paint beautiful works of art depicting the lives of the holiest people and for each Christian to keep an icon or artwork of their patron saint. By gazing on these things, they kept a clear vision of a holy life in their eyes; as a result, they were motivated to be holy too. Of course, above all else, Scripture teaches us to "fix our eyes upon Jesus, the author and finisher of our faith" (Hebrews 12:2). This is the rationale behind the Catholic practice of adoration (that I mentioned earlier), which takes place when a believer quietly sits (or kneels) in the presence of the Eucharist and lovingly gazes at it. The Church understands that what we look at, we love. What we love, we will be like!

That's the power of vision and visualization. It's not just a sound practice for self-development and success. It's a powerful spiritual principle and practice founded upon undeniable ancient truth.

In your quest to pursue your God-given potential, don't forget to *seek to see*. Seek a vision of God for your life, as well as the life you want to live for God. Practice visualization, both for success—and for saintliness.

QUESTIONS FOR REFLECTION

• Have you spent time cultivating a vision of God by meditating on Scripture, reflecting on nature, or observing and reflecting on the life of a godly person? What's your plan for doing that?

• Do you understand the difference between a self-centered approach to visualization, which is just "imagining things I want," and a God-centered approach to visualization, which is visualizing who God wants you to become and what great work he wants you to accomplish? Do you understand the difference? The former is about self-improvement for your own selfish gain. The latter is about fulfilling your potential for the glory of God and good of the world. Take time to think about that.

• Who is someone you can "take note of" as an example of both success and saintliness? Take time today to figure out who you can look to as an example to follow.

RECOMMENDED RESOURCES

• *Knowing God* by J. I. Packer

• *The Evidential Power of Beauty: Science and Theology Meet* by Thomas Dubay

• *The Talent Code: Greatness Isn't Born. It's Grown. Here's How.* by Daniel Coyle

Chapter Six

TAKE IT "BIRD BY BIRD"

"I'm not smarter or more talented than anyone else. I don't have access to resources that you don't. Every day, I identify the critical tasks I need to do to move forward toward my goals; and by the end of the day, I do them." **—Andy Frisella, when people ask him how he built a nine-figure business**

"Remember that nothing is small in the eyes of God. Do all you do with great love." **—Saint Therese of Lisieux**

Are you overwhelmed by the enormity of a challenge or problem—either in your personal life or in the world at large? Does the prospect of pursuing your full, God-given potential overwhelm you?

Years ago, I read Anne Lamott's great book *Bird by Bird: Some Thoughts on Writing and Life.* Though I don't agree with Lamott on everything, I have always respected her as someone who possesses helpful insight into not only the craft of writing well but also the art of living well. She is also one of the wittiest women alive, so when I picked up the book I looked forward to what I thought was going to be the funny anecdote in which she explained the story behind the title.

It turns out the story isn't funny at all—but it is extremely insightful.

Lamott explains that, when her older brother was ten

years old, his elementary school required him to write a substantial research paper on the topic of his choice. He chose birds. In order to meet his teacher's requirements, his project had to cover several birds and go into depth about each of them, providing not only descriptions of characteristics and behavior but also illustrations.

As you can imagine, such a project would demand that you start early in the semester, diligently set aside time each day to work, and not let yourself get behind. As most kids do, Lamott's brother procrastinated and allowed the work to fall behind. When the deadline loomed a mere day away, he shifted into full panic mode.

In the middle of his breakdown, their father put his arm around her brother and said, "Bird by bird, buddy. Just take it bird by bird."

Most people think the term "writer" is code for someone who's lazy and unemployed. The reality is, writing—good writing—is time-consuming and excruciatingly hard to do. It is mentally and even physically exhausting. The idea of writing a full-length book is so overwhelming that professional writers often share stories of the creative ways they rationalize not actually sitting down and getting started. (In a stroke of irony, I found this chapter to be the hardest one to write. By the time I arrived at this part of the manuscript, I'd begun to feel overwhelmed. "I'm only on chapter six! I still have eleven chapters to go!")

Lamott's advice to take it "bird by bird" means, in practical terms: focus on short assignments and (*I quote*) "shitty first drafts." Choose a small step and just take your best swing at it—bad as it may be. In the end, consistency and revision will be what help you achieve your big goal.

This advice is 100 percent applicable not only to writers but to anyone's life—and it's supported by principles and examples found all over the Bible and the lives of saintly men and women throughout history.

I like that Lamott's example involves birds. It provides a nice connection to something Jesus said in Matthew 30:29–31. In the preceding verses, he calls on his disciples to be fearless—which includes not getting overwhelmed by what they have to accomplish and the challenges they'll face. To explain why they shouldn't stress out, Jesus says, "Are not two sparrows sold for a penny? Yet not one of them will fall to the ground apart from the will of your Father. And even the very hairs of your head are all numbered. So do not worry; you are worth more than many sparrows!"

Essentially, Jesus's argument is this: "Listen, don't be overwhelmed. You are loved by a God who pays careful attention to things that most people consider unimportant and insignificant. He is a God of meticulous detail when it comes to taking care of you, even down to the number of hairs on your head." (If you've seen a photo of me, you know that God doesn't have many strands to keep track of!) He may be running the whole universe—with its one billion trillion stars (and way too many species of snakes . . . not a fan)—but nothing gets past him. He never drops the ball. He gives personal, singular, full-hearted attention to everything going on in all of reality.

As staggering as it is to believe, God may govern all the

heavens and the earth—but he still takes things "bird by bird."

Scripture also uniformly testifies that God delights in small beginnings. The whole human race began with one man and one woman. The Church—which has members from every tribe, tongue, and nation in the world—began with twelve blue-collar fishermen. God praises those who perform small, seemingly insignificant acts, such as the woman who only gave half a penny to the offering (Mark 12:41–44; Luke 21:1–4). He likes to win wars with small bands confronting overwhelming odds (Judges 7; 1 Maccabees 3:19). He explains that even those whose faith is "small" like a mustard seed can move mountains (Matthew 13:31–32; Mark 4:30–32; Luke 13:18–19). God doesn't just delight in single acts—he even goes after single, isolated people. He'll sweep the house to find one coin. He'll leave the flock to find one lamb. He'll run away from his house in joy to embrace one son who was lost, but now is found (Luke 15).

God loves small. He loves minute details. He loves the one.

That's why God is so effective—in his power, in his providence, and in his love. God's "little" actions compound universally—across time and space—and result in this vibrant, wild, and wonderful world in which we live.

People like us, who aspire to great faith and gritty mental toughness, need to follow suit. We need to realize that even our smallest acts can and will compound to great power and effect. So every day, we need to commit ourselves to identifying the critical tasks that will move us forward piece by piece—not only in crushing our goals, but in coming closer to God.

Saint Therese of Lisieux is a Roman Catholic saint that people of all faiths and traditions love and admire. The Catholic Church considers her a patron saint of missions and evangelism. Over the centuries, she has impacted millions and millions of people. Yet she never left her little Carmelite convent in France and died at the young age of twenty-four. What was the secret to her spiritual power and influence?

She called it her "Little Way."

"I do small acts with great love."

Critical tasks + every day = success.

Small acts + great love = saintliness.

If you want to be a man or woman of great faith with gritty mental toughness, understand that you are greatly loved by a God of meticulous details; a God who loves the small, the one, and values you "far more than sparrows."

Understand that. Embrace that.

Then take it "bird by bird."

QUESTIONS FOR REFLECTION

• If you have a task in front of you that looks too big to complete, take some time to break it down into its components. What are individual steps that you can accomplish easily and industriously?

• Do you ever take time to appreciate the small things in your life, whether it's tiny kindnesses and blessings or just little details you never noticed before?

RECOMMENDED RESOURCES

- *St. Benedict and St. Therese: The Little Rule and the Little Way* by Fr. Dwight Longenecker

- *The Practice of the Presence of God* by Brother Lawrence

Chapter Seven

FOLLOW THE PATTERN

"Without a serious effort to live ordinary Christianity, there is no possibility of extraordinary Christianity." **—Father Jonathan Robinson**

"Success leaves clues." **—Tony Robbins**

"I'm Luke Skywalker. I'm here to rescue you."

As I sat in a movie theater in downtown Lincoln, Nebraska, those eight words stirred a desire in my soul for the first time: the longing to be a hero. As I watched a movie that had just hit theaters in May 1977, the movie that would soon become a force in American culture and part of the very fabric of my childhood, I was enchanted. I marveled as a farm boy from a desert planet liberated a beautiful princess, destroyed the menacing Death Star, and began his journey to becoming a Jedi Knight, a noble protector of the galaxy and a guardian of peace and justice. *Star Wars* gave me a new hope that I, an ordinary kid from the Midwest, could become someone extraordinary.

That theme of an *ordinary person becoming extraordinary* runs through many of the movies that stir our hearts to become heroes. Just as Luke Skywalker was a lowly moisture farmer on Tatooine, Peter Parker was a nerdy student who was bullied by his classmates (*Spider-Man*). When he wasn't operating as a hacker, Neo lived a double life as the ordinary citizen Thomas Anderson (*The Matrix*). The little Simba, while he was heir to the throne in the Pride Lands, spent most of his adolescence exiled from his kingdom (*The Lion King*). Frodo the hobbit lived comfortably in the Shire, enjoying potatoes, ale, and pipes far from any kind of adventure (*The Lord of the Rings*). And of course, Harry Potter, possibly the most iconic hero of the Millennial generation, lived in a cupboard under the stairs at 4 Privet Drive. Humble beginnings lead to epic endings.

But there's more to it than that. Not only do these movies share one theme in common, they also share a structure that, according to American mythologist Joseph Campbell, can be found in virtually every great hero story, in every culture of the world, down through the ages. Once life begins in the ordinary world, there is:

A Call to Adventure	R2-D2 gives Luke a message from Princess Leia
The Refusal of the Call	Peter Parker uses his power for his own selfish gain—to win wrestling matches and earn money
A Meeting with a Mentor	Morpheus tells Neo to take the red pill
A Crossing of a Threshold	The Fellowship set off on their journey to Mount Doom

And so on . . .

Don't miss the point: All the ordinary people in these stories are individuals with different backstories, life settings, personalities, and talents. They are unique. But the way an epic story unfolds in their lives follows a remarkably similar structure that leads them from ordinary person to extraordinary hero.

Guess what? This is true of every man or woman who ever wanted to fulfill their God-given potential . . .

. . . to become a person of excellence or success, or a giant of faith with a passionate heart, powerful mind, and strong will.

The Hero's Journey can seem like a storytelling "hack" at first—a shortcut to character development and compelling tales that, if inserted into a story, guarantees its resonance and popularity. But there's a difference between a form—a framework that requires understanding and effort to grasp and successfully use—and a formula—plugging the same beats into an outline and expecting it to artificially generate success. The difference between the two is the difference between *Star Wars* and its hundreds of less successful clones that still saturate the market to this day.

The same is true for living a life of excellence and pursuing your potential. There is no secret formula known only to a select few that, when plugged in, will guarantee reward. There is no spiritual "gimmick" or magical, supernatural experience you can discover that will allow you to bypass the fundamental practices that lead someone to improve themselves—whether we're talking about becoming a better preacher or football player. But there is a standard pattern for success. That's true for personal development, and it's also true in the spiritual life. While you may be utterly unique in the eyes of God, how you become more like God is not.

Consider the men and women across the centuries, from every great Christian tradition and denomination, who impacted the world for Christ, and you will discover the same "clues" to their success. Among other things:

- they pray (1 Thessalonians 5:16–18)

- they take Communion (John 6:53–59; Mark 14:22–25; Acts 20:7; 1 Corinthians 11:23–26)

- they study and reflect on the Word of God (Psalm 1; Psalm 19; Acts 17:11; Hebrews 4:12)

- they confess their sins (1 John 1:9; James 5:16)

- they dedicate themselves to regular times of worship (Jeremiah 20:13; John 4:21–24; Hebrews 12:28–29)

- they cultivate thankfulness (Psalm 9:1; Ephesians 5:18–20; Colossians 2:6–7)

- they use their money for God-honoring purposes (Proverbs 3:9; Matthew 6:21; Acts 4:34; 2 Corinthians 9:6–7; 1 Timothy 6:17–19;)

- they serve the poor and oppressed and commit themselves to love and good works (Proverbs 3:27–29; Proverbs 28:27; Isaiah 58:6–11; Matthew 5:15–16; 1 John 3:17)

- they commit to a local church (Exodus 20:8–11; Acts 2:42; Hebrews 10:24–25)

Saint Francis of Assisi. D. L. Moody. Saint Therese of Lisieux. William Wilberforce. Dietrich Bonhoeffer. C. S. Lewis. Mother Theresa. Billy Graham. Saint John Paul the Great. None of them discovered some sort of alternative, esoteric path to spiritual greatness, and none of them were able to fake it by following a few superficial steps.

All of them made use of the ordinary means of growing in God's grace and holiness, and that is how they became extraordinary saints and exceptional men and women of God.

If you want to follow in the footsteps of those who exemplified godliness, greatness, and grit, you have to reject the idea that there's a "secret prayer" or "special program" that will fast-track you to overnight spiritual success.

There isn't.

You also have to stop worrying that you will invest time in your spiritual life, go to great effort to follow the preordained path, and not see results.

That won't happen.

Of course, I'm not saying that there won't be struggles and setbacks. Of course there will. Remember what I wrote earlier: faith is a battle! But the Scriptures are clear that "he has given you everything you need for life and godliness" (1 Peter 1:3). God promises us: "You will seek me and find me, when you seek me with all of your heart" (Jeremiah 29:13). And Jesus was very clear that our actions get a response from God: "Ask, and it will be given to you; seek and you will find; knock and the door will be opened to you" (Matthew 7:7).

So it really comes down to this. You're looking for another

way because you want to avoid putting in the work of cultivating real devotion to God.

You're questioning the effectiveness of practices that, guided by the Holy Spirit, have transformed countless ordinary people into extraordinary saints.

But the reality is that there is nothing deficient or ineffective about any of the God-ordained, time-tested methods of becoming more like Jesus.

What is deficient is our commitment.

We have not felt the effects of prayer and Scripture and Communion in our lives because we have not really dedicated ourselves to them.

Stop looking for the next thing. Stop doubting that you can become a truly godly person. Start using the gifts and tools God has given you.

Follow the pattern. Fulfill your potential.

Go all in.

"Take hold of that for which Christ Jesus took hold of you" (Philippians 3:12–14).

Embrace the proven process.

Do the work.

Trust God that you'll get the results.

QUESTIONS FOR REFLECTION

• Has there been a time when you tried to coast through a process by superficially repeating its steps, only to understand that you had to truly grasp the fundamentals before it would work for you? Can you identify a place in your spiritual life where you are doing that?

• What's a faith story that truly resonates with you? Is there a way you could investigate its framework and try to use it in your own life? In other words, is there a pattern in the life of a saint or holy man or woman that you could imitate—not to become a carbon copy of that saint, but to use their life as a reliable pattern for your own spiritual development?

• Take inventory of your own spiritual life. How much does your life conform to the "standard framework" of holiness? What "best practices" do you need to add and work hard to develop in order to grow in faith, hope, and love?

RECOMMENDED RESOURCES

• *The Imitation of Christ* by Thomas à Kempis

• *The Purpose Driven Life: What on Earth Am I Here For?* by Rick Warren

• *Butler's Lives of the Saints: Concise, Modernized Edition* edited by Bernard Bangley

• *More Than Conquerors: Portraits of Believers from All Walks of Life* by John Woodbridge

Chapter Eight

EMBRACE MOTIVATING GRACE

"Few souls understand what God would accomplish
in them if they were to abandon themselves unre-
servedly to Him and if they were to allow His grace to
mold them accordingly." —**Saint Ignatius Loyola**

"Through many dangers, toils, and snares
I have already come
'Tis grace hath brought me safe thus far,
And grace will lead me home."

—**"Amazing Grace," John Newton**

My grandfather Richard Frederick Lotter, whom we called Pop-Pop Dick, was a factory worker and custodian for most of his life. Although he never earned a lot of money, I remember him as rich in generosity—and always kind and patient with his grandchildren.

I also remember him coughing—a lot. After years of inhaling smoke and chemicals, he developed emphysema, and by the time he came to live with us the summer of my fifth-grade year, it was killing him. Eventually he got so weak he could hardly move—except to slink in and out of bed to use the portable toilet in his room. The Porta Potty.

One day, my mom asked me to empty that toilet. It was a

55

simple task, really—just dumping a bucket into the toilet in our bathroom. "Simple," however, did not mean it was pleasant, and I dug in my heels and grumbled. "That's gross," I protested. "Why do I have to do that?"

"Do it," my mom replied. "And be quiet—if Pop-Pop hears you, he'll feel like he's a burden on us."

I knew that was true. I think Pop-Pop was embarrassed that he had to be served. But that didn't change the fact that I walked into his room irritated, indignant that I had perform so menial—and fecal—a task. I deserved better.

Though I entered the room in full brat mode, I managed to stealthily mask my pouting—or so I thought. Once I had emptied the bucket and returned it to the Porta Potty, Pop-Pop called me over. "Hey, Vaughn," he said. "C'mere for a second."

Okay, Pop-Pop. What do you want?

He smiled at me through his coughing. "Emptying that pot. It's gross, isn't it?"

My heart took the escalator into my throat.

Oh no, I thought. *He heard what I said to Mom.*

I braced for a lecture, a tongue lashing. I don't know why, since that wasn't like Pop-Pop at all—I think I realized I deserved one. But instead of a blow, I heard:

"I'm sorry you had to do that. *Thank you*. I appreciate it."

Thank you? Pop-Pop's response to my complaining was . . . gratitude?

But Pop-Pop wasn't done. He stretched out his arm, still lean and muscular from all those years of factory work. His hand was closed tight, holding something. He motioned for me to hold out my own hand; not really understanding, I slid my open palm under his closed fist.

Slowly, weakly, he opened up his fingers, and I felt something folded and papery and crisp fall into my palm. I took it and then looked down.

It was a five-dollar bill.

Five dollars! Am I dreaming?

That was 1985, not 2021! Taking inflation and various other economic factors into account, five dollars back then would be worth *a lot more* today. Probably . . . like . . .

A BILLION DOLLARS.

Okay, maybe not—but that's what it felt like at the time. Five dollars could almost buy you *two* G.I. Joe figures. It was only $2.99 short of the price of the A-Team Moving Target Game. And good Lord, do you know how many Pixy Stix and Razzles I could purchase with *five guacamoles*? My candy supply would be funded through the end the month! The year! Heck, the end of Reagan's second term!

As I reveled in my bounty, my grandfather spoke up again:

"Thanks again, Vaughn," he said. "I think you are a *great* grandson."

A . . . great . . . grandson?

That's when it hit me. My grandfather had responded to my complaint with thanksgiving. My reprobate attitude had been met with reward.

I couldn't have told you—at that very moment—what had brought conviction to my heart and melted it. But I felt it. And every time I think of this story, I am *still moved to tears.*

Because in that moment, Pop-Pop exhibited what we need from God more than anything else.

It's what the world needs from *us* more than anything else. And it's what you need more than anything to drive you toward pursuing your full potential, pressing on when you falter and fail and recovering quickly when you make a mess of your life.

Grace.

The Bible talks about grace all over the place.

"For by grace you have been saved; and this not of yourselves. It is the gift of God" (Ephesians 2:8).

"Let us then with confidence draw near to the throne of grace, that we may receive mercy and find grace to help in time of need" (Hebrews 4:16).

"And God is able to make all grace abound to you, so that having all sufficiency in all things at all times, you may abound in every good work" (2 Corinthians 9:8).

"But by the grace of God I am what I am, and his grace toward me was not in vain. On the contrary, I worked harder than any of them, though it was not I, but the grace of God that is with me" (Saint Paul quoted in 1 Corinthians 15:10).

Jesus never used the word "grace," but he lived it.

He extended the grace of healing to those suffering from sickness.

He extended the grace of forgiveness to those struggling in sin.

He extended the grace of his power to those oppressed and possessed by demons.

He even asked God to show grace to those who nailed him to the cross.

The cross itself was the ultimate act of grace. On it, the King of Glory gave his life for those who hated and rejected him. It was the most perfect expression of God's love for his enemies.

Grace is unmerited favor. Something richer and greater than mercy: that which responds to aggression and hostility with undeserved kindness and lavish love.

Of all the passages in Scripture that extol the grace of God, my favorite is Jesus's story of the Prodigal Son (Luke 15:11–24). To summarize it very briefly: Jesus says that there were two sons. One day, the younger son went to his father and asked for his inheritance—basically saying, "I want my money more than I want a relationship with you. I'll live as if you were dead." The father generously agreed, at which point the younger son went off into the world and squandered all the money that had been given to him. After hitting rock bottom, he ended up working in a pigsty, which for ancient Jews was about as unclean and detestable a fate as you could experience.

Finally, the son came to his senses and thought, "I have to go home." He figured he'd return with his tail between his legs and grovel. Assuming his father had already disowned him as a son, he came up with a speech to try to persuade his dad to just let him work as a hired hand.

When the son arrived home, what happened next would have been surprising—no, shocking, even scandalous—to the original listeners.

According to Jewish custom, there was only one time a father was really "allowed" to run: that was in battle. Otherwise, it was considered beneath his dignity. A noble father stays put, and people come to him!

Guess what happened in Jesus's story? The father saw his son returning home . . .

. . . and he ran to welcome him back!

He ran!

What's even more mind-blowing: when the son began his little speech about becoming a hired hand, his father would have none of it. He was so delirious that his son had returned that he put the best clothes on him, slid a gold ring onto his finger (a sign of belonging), and called for household-wide celebration.

The older brother—the goodie two-shoes of the family, who'd stayed behind to work on the estate while his brother squandered his money—was furious. He couldn't believe the father was showing such mercy, such generosity, such grace!

But the father responded: "My son [. . .] you are always with me, and everything I have is yours. But we had to celebrate and be glad, because this brother of yours was dead and is alive again; he was lost and is found" (15:31–32).

What incredible mercy.

What incredible grace!

Do you understand that Jesus is saying? *This is what God is like! This is how he relates to us!*

It doesn't matter how weak we are.

It doesn't matter if we've disgraced him and his name.

It doesn't matter if we've made a train wreck of our lives.

When we turn to him, or *return* to him, he runs to us! He puts the best clothes on our back and the best shoes on our feet. He puts a ring on our finger and calls for a celebration!

God hears us complaining and whining about emptying the Porta Potty. And he gives us five dollars.

Scratch that.

He gives us five MILLION dollars. That's how overwhelming and overflowing his grace is.

So now do you understand a little better the significance of Saint Paul's words in 1 Corinthians 15:10?

> But by the grace of God I am what I am, and his grace toward me was not in vain. *On the contrary, I worked harder than any of them, though it was not I, but the grace of God that is with me* [emphasis mine].

Out of sheer, delirious, intoxicated gratitude for the grace of God, Saint Paul "worked harder" than anyone else, passionately driven to make the most of his life. He knew that the grace of God would sustain him through good times and bad, through successes and failures, in epic battles with the devil and knockout rounds with the sin in his own heart.

Over the course of my life, I have read academic explanations of God's grace and listened to sermons and lectures delivered by learned preachers and theologians. But nothing has stayed with me, or left a more significant impact on my soul, than God's grace given to me in the form of a crisp five-dollar-bill. In fact, time after time, as I have found myself slow to trust God and hesitant to move forward smartly and unafraid, I've visualized Pop-Pop Dick giving me payment and praise I didn't earn or deserve—and I remembered that the little bit of grace my grandfather extended to me that day is but a drop in the vast ocean of grace that our Heavenly Father pours out on me—on us—every moment of our lives.

The blazing nuclear power at the center of Saint Paul's life, my life, and yours is God's grace. The very foundation of our sacred drive, our ability to be focused, disciplined, gritty, confident, hopeful, and tenacious in the pursuit of our potential—is God's unparalleled mercy and love.

When we really understand how much *God is for us*, we know that nothing can stand against us . . .

. . . and nothing can stop us.

That's the key to becoming a God-called, grace-driven force of nature and force for good in the world.

Accept it. And take action!

You understand?

God's grace is everything.

Accept it, and you'll find the motivation to pursue your potential.

Embrace it, and you'll be able to do anything.

QUESTIONS FOR REFLECTION

- Charles Spurgeon said, "For every one time I look at my own sin, I look ten times at the cross of Christ." If you are struggling with still beating yourself up for past sins, when was the last time you stopped obsessing about your own failures and focused on the amazing grace that Jesus extends to you? Take ten minutes this week to meditate on Matthew 25:32–56, the crucifixion of Jesus, and ask God to ignite your heart with the realization that Christ died for you—and loves you more than you can possibly imagine.

• We experience God's grace most profoundly when we extend it to others. In a culture where people are constantly criticizing one another, fault-finding, and—in general—being pretty terrible to one another, how can you show grace to someone who doesn't "deserve" it? Pray that God reveals some way you can show someone radical, relentless grace this week.

• You've heard of "random acts of kindness?" When I was a youth pastor, I used to take my kids out to perform "random acts of grace." I challenge you to do something we did all the time (with great success): Go into a restaurant. Order less than five dollars' worth of food. Then give the server a ridiculously ginormous tip. (I'm talking twenty-five to fifty dollars or more.) Explain to them that God has shown you lavish grace and divine generosity that you didn't deserve, and that you just wanted to pass it on. :)

RECOMMENDED RESOURCES

• *What's So Amazing About Grace?* by Philip Yancey

• *The Name of God is Mercy* by Pope Francis

• *God's Healing Mercy: Finding Your Path to Forgiveness, Peace, and Joy* by Kathleen Beckman

• *The Confessions* by Saint Augustine, translated by Sr. Maria Boulding O.S.B., Vintage Spiritual Classics Edition

• *On the Road with St. Augustine: A Real-World Spirituality for Restless Hearts* by James K. A. Smith

Chapter Nine

PLAY YOUR NOTE

"And we know that for those who love God all things work together for good, for those who are called according to his purpose." —**Romans 8:28**

"Romans 8:28 doesn't say 'we understand' how all things work together for good. It says 'we know.' So would you get past 'understanding' and get on to 'knowing'? Understand it or not! I don't understand how a black cow eats green grass and gives white milk, but I still love ice cream!" —**Vance Havner**

My dad died in November 2014, but when he was alive, he was an amazing pianist. After graduating with a degree in music performance from Houghton College in 1969, he spent his life first as a music professor, then as a piano and organ salesman. Throughout the years, he gave concert after concert, performing everything from Chopin's "Revolutionary Etude" on the piano to Charles-Marie Widor's "Toccata" on the pipe organ. What I liked best, however, was when we'd have a special worship service at our church and my dad would take requests. He would perform stirring renditions of the greatest hymns throughout the ages, the congregation erupting in "Amen" after "Amen." No one played "Great Is Thy Faithfulness" like my dad.

While I did not follow in his footsteps as an adult, I did take piano lessons when I was a little boy. When I was five years old, I participated in a recital with roughly a hundred other students, in a large recital hall that seated well over five hundred people. In the front of the hall, up on the stage, was a big, beautiful Steinway grand piano.

For my piece, I had to perform a duet with my dad. I don't remember exactly what song I was supposed to play, but it was a basic tune. Exceedingly basic. Something like "Twinkle, Twinkle, Little Star" or "Mary Had a Little Lamb." I don't even think there were any chords involved. All I had to do was play one single note at a time.

Despite this, I was extremely nervous. My mouth was dry, my palms wet with sweat, my stomach fluttering. Looking out into the smiling but intimidating audience, I needed one more round of reassurances from my dad.

I looked up at him and, earnestly as any son has ever spoken to his father, asked, "Dad . . .

". . . are you sure you can do this?"

The audience heard and burst into laughter.

If the notion that a thirtysomething music performance major and lifelong concert pianist couldn't handle a selection from *Teaching Little Fingers to Play* amused Dad, however, he didn't show it. "Yes," he replied with a nod and a smile. "I think we've got this."

With that, I played my first note. Then my second. Then my third. Sometimes I played the next note too fast, sometimes not fast enough. Occasionally, I hit the wrong note altogether.

It didn't matter. Because shortly after I started, my father placed his left hand on the keyboard, then put his arm around me and placed his right hand there too. He started playing a flourish of notes and chords, and suddenly, my one-note effort was transformed into a performance worthy of a standing ovation.

I contributed very, very little to that performance; but together, my dad and I made beautiful music.

Too often in life, we believe that success is determined by our effort alone. While it's important and essential to take (as Jocko says) "extreme ownership" of our lives and actions, we need to recognize what is our responsibility and what is not, what is within our control and what is beyond it.

In the worlds of entrepreneurship, self-help, and success, it's common to hear that it's our job to work hard and produce results. From a practical point of view, that is true. We can't simply be passive and idle and hope good things will happen. We have to be intentional, aggressive, and tenacious; if we are, we can be confident that the outcome is going to be positive, or that at the very least we can take pride in a job well done.

But from a spiritual perspective, there's a simple reason we are absolutely not responsible for guaranteeing results: we are not God. We are not all-knowing and all-powerful. We don't see all of life as a whole, only parts of our own life. There are so many factors and forces beyond our control—dynamics of the universe that God can handle but we, as finite and imperfect human beings, cannot. If we think we can, we will become disappointed and discouraged at best; at worst, we'll drive ourselves to insanity and suicide.

No, our job is not to produce results. Instead, it is to be

faithful. It is our duty to wake up every day and, as my friend (best-selling author and elite performance coach) Ben Newman says, "attack the process." That means it is our job to act, to execute, to do what we know we are supposed to do to the best of our abilities, and to trust that God will bless our efforts.

Take a moment to really consider these verses about what's referred to as God's providence—his ability to work all things for his purposes and for our good:

> Remember the former things, those of long ago;
> I am God, and there is no other;
> I am God, and there is none like me.
> I make known the end from the beginning,
> from ancient times, what is still to come.
> I say, "My purpose will stand,
> and I will do all that I please."
> From the east I summon a bird of prey;
> from a far-off land, a man to fulfill my purpose.
> What I have said, that I will bring about;
> what I have planned, that I will do.
>
> (Isaiah 46:9–11)

> For I know that the Lord is great, and that our Lord is above all gods. Whatever the Lord pleases, he does, in heaven and on earth, in the seas and all deeps. He is who makes the clouds rise at the end of the earth, who makes lightnings for the rain and brings forth the wind from his storehouses.
>
> (Psalm 135:5–7)

The eyes of all look to You, and You give them their food in season. You open your hand and satisfy the desire of every living thing.

(Psalm 145:15–16)

All the inhabitants of the earth are accounted as nothing, and he does according to his will among the host of heaven and among the inhabitants of the earth; and none can stay his hand or say to him, "What have you done?"

(Daniel 4:35)

Are not two sparrows sold for a penny? And not one of them will fall to the ground apart from your Father.

(Matthew 10:29)

Continue to work out your salvation with fear and trembling, *for it is God who works in you to will and to act in order to fulfill his good purpose.*
(Philippians 2:12–13; emphasis mine)

That last verse is especially relevant to what I've been saying.

We do the work. But he is the one who determines the results.

We control what we can control. But we entrust the uncontrollable to the Almighty.

Properly understood, this truth should fill you with an

overwhelming happiness, an indescribable peace, and an unshakeable confidence.

It means all you have to do on a daily basis is play your one note. God our Father will put his arms on either side of you and turn the events of your life into a beautiful piece of music that will captivate and impact the world.

It means that even if you screw up, all you have to do is keep playing your one note. God our Father will put his arms on either side of you and deliver such an impressive performance that your mistake, your wrong move, will not ruin the music. In fact, it will sound as though it belonged there all along.

It means that all you have to do when you attempt to achieve a huge, larger-than-life, laughably "unrealistic" goal is keep playing one note at a time, hour after hour, day after day. God our Father will put his arms on either side of you and play such an expert, perfect combination of keys and chords that the final performance will far exceed your tiny contribution.

That's the mindset that will help you *consistently* pursue your God-given potential.

That's the way of thinking that will drive your willingness to act.

That's the attitude that will power your persistence and help you fulfill God's purpose for your life.

Play your note . . .

. . . and let God put his arms on either side of you and do the rest.

QUESTIONS FOR REFLECTION

• What does it look like for you to faithfully "attack the process" in your life right now? What are the things you know you need to do to move forward toward your goals? Take time to write those down and evaluate how you're doing.

• If nothing else, I think being faithful means three things: *loving, learning,* and *laboring.* Each day, ask yourself these three questions:

   o   Am I showing people love? (1 Corinthians 13)
   o   Am I investing time in my own education and self-development? (The word *disciple* in the Bible literally means "learner.")
   o   Am I working hard to be productive? (Ecclesiastes 9:10; Colossians 3:23–24)

RECOMMENDED RESOURCES

• *Trustful Surrender to Divine Providence: The Secret of Peace and Happiness* by Father Jean Baptiste Saint-Jure

• *Trusting God* by Jerry Bridges

• *Ruthless Trust: The Ragamuffin's Path to God* by Brennan Manning

• *The Way of Trust and Love: A Retreat Guided by St. Therese of Lisieux* by Father Jacques Philippe

Chapter Ten

CONFESS TO CRUSH

"The confession of evil works is the first beginning of good works." —**Saint Augustine**

"The righteous are bold as a lion." —**Proverbs 28:1b**

Draped in a black vampire cape, my eleven-year-old
brother Lance crept outside my basement bedroom. His
eyebrows sloped downward, his beady brown eyes peering
at the closed wooden door with the intensity of Dracula. A
nefarious grin spread across his face as he imagined the situation inside: Vaughn and his girlfriend, Shelley.[1] Alone in his
bedroom. Against the rules.

It was the spring of 1990. I was seventeen years old, dating a freshman cheerleader, and certainly not unaware of my
little brother's schemes. Like most pesky little brothers, he
liked to snoop and spy on his older brother—especially when
it came to my love life. Unusually, however, Lance liked to do
it dressed as Nosferatu, Lord of the Undead.

But I thought I had the perfect plan to ward off the little
bloodsucker. Just as a vampire recoiled at the Cross of Christ,
Lance could be repelled by invoking the Name Above All Names.

---

1 I have changed my high school girlfriend's name to "Shelley" to pro-
tect her anonymity. That's not her real name. :)

"Hey, bro, listen," I said to him earlier in the day. "I'm going to hang out with Shelley in my room, okay?"

"Insolent fool," he replied. "You can't. It's against the rules. I'm going to tell Mom and Dad."

I put my arm around him. "Yeah, yeah, I know. Normally, you're right. But this time, I have a very special reason."

"Pathetic im-be-cile," he said with a sneer. "Okay. What is it?"

I paused, clothing my face with earnestness.

"I'm going to tell Shelley about Jesus."

Lance thought about it for a moment.

As he did, a pang of guilt hit my heart. I knew full well that my motives weren't spiritual. They weren't noble or mission driven or in any way motivated by true love for Shelley.

They were motivated by hormones.

Nevertheless, I continued.

"Look, she really needs Jesus. You can't say anything to Mom or Dad because Shelley's probably really sensitive and would be embarrassed because of her sins. You know what I mean?"

Ugh. Who was the one who needed to be embarrassed by their sins? Shelley was actually a very sweet, churchgoing girl who cared deeply about other people. There was as much evidence (if not more) in her life that she had a relationship with God as there was in mine. Who was I to judge her?

As I pondered that, I felt the weight of my own uneasy conscience grow heavier. It looked like I was going to successfully fool my little brother. But I was acting like a fool in the process.

"Okay, fine," Lance finally conceded. "I won't sneak in. Probably."

Instead of backing off my plan, I doubled down on my deception.

"Lance, listen to me," I'd put on my best stern face. "It is very important that you don't sneak in and interrupt us. Extremely important. You understand why?"

"Kind of. Why, fool?"

I took a deep breath.

By this time, my inner moral compass was whirring and spinning, and a little voice (the Holy Spirit?) was shouting "Warning! Warning! Danger, Will Robinson!" trying to get me to reverse course.

It was no good.

"What if I'm in the middle of sharing the gospel and you barge in?" I'd asked. "Do you want to mess up the work of the Holy Spirit?"

Lance looked at me and clenched his teeth, his expression alternating between sympathy and skepticism.

"Fine, foo-el," he'd said. "I get it. I won't spy on you. I promise."

All too easy, I thought to myself, echoing Darth Vader.

The threat had been neutralized. But I had given myself over to the Dark Side.

Later that afternoon, my mom safely occupied with chores upstairs on the other end of the house, I led Shelley into my bedroom and shut the door.

Now, to be fair to myself, I was a genuine, bona fide Christian young man. I really did want to love Jesus and tell others about him. But my faith and convictions were, at that time, a wee bit inconsistent—or maybe a way bit. Thus, whatever spiritual conversation Shelley and I began that afternoon quickly degenerated into a rollicking good time of (un)holy kisses.

It wasn't X-rated, mind you. Or even R-rated. But I knew that I wasn't living up to the standards that I professed. I knew that I was doing something in private that I had condemned in public. At that moment, there was a continental divide between what I had preached and what I was practicing.

I was a fake. A poser. A hypocrite. And I knew it. I understood that so acutely that, to be frank, the whole escapade wasn't as enjoyable as I hoped it would be. After all, it's hard to feel good when you don't feel good about yourself—and you are justified in feeling that way!

The good news was that at least I was the only one who was going to know what a duplicitous loser I was.

Right?

I mean, while I had not taken great pains to preserve my integrity, I had been very careful to avoid being found out.

My plan was foolproof, my strategy superb—I had already lied to my little brother, but just to be safe, I perched a little brass elephant (one my grandfather had given me) on the doorknob. It had a little bell inside it. If Lance tried to stealthily turn the knob, open the door, and creep inside undetected, the falling, tinkling elephant would give me all the warning I'd need.

That's what I thought.

To my surprise, our carnal carousing ended very soon after it began. It was rudely, sharply, startlingly interrupted by a prepubescent denizen of the underworld. A sneaky soul-sucker thrilled to stick it to his older brother.

Ah-HA!

I thought I had devised a foolproof plan, a fail-safe in the event that curiosity and conniving got the better of Lance. I was wrong—not just about my plan, but about his. There was no stealth or sneakiness in Lance's approach at all.

He just came crashing through the door.

Disoriented and discombobulated, I pushed Shelley off me and jumped up from the bed. Lance's cape swirled around him as he cackled with nefarious glee.

"Oh ho HO!" he said. And then, sounding like the Riddler from the 1960s Batman show, he spoke five words that have been indelibly etched into my conscience ever since.

"Telling her about JESUS, EHHHH?"

I turned away from Lance and looked over at Shelley, hoping she wouldn't put two and two together. But the moment I saw her expression, I knew she had. The jig was up.

"Telling . . . me . . . about . . . Jesus?" she said slowly and softly.

If that whole scene had been an episode of *Looney Tunes* and I were Daffy Duck, I would have—at that moment—turned into a donkey. I certainly felt like an ass.

My embarrassment quickly turned to fury, but it was too late. By the time I realized I wanted to drive a stake through my little brother's heart, Lance was halfway up the stairs and seconds away from alerting my mother to my sins.

"Mom! Mom!" I could hear him yelling from upstairs. "Vaughn was telling Shelley about Jesus! With his TONGUE!"

I took a deep breath, realizing that I'd probably be grounded for months. Yet the worst punishment was seeing the look on Shelley's face. It wasn't a look of anger as much as disbelief and disappointment:

You told your brother you'd be talking with me about Jesus?

So you lied to him.

You are also telling other people I need Jesus when you are clearly going against your own conscience and lying about making out with me.

You have zero problem using me for your physical pleasure, but you think I'm going to hell.

She looked betrayed—like Jesus after Judas's kiss.

Many years later, I'm glad the look on Shelley's face has stayed with me. It reminds me how people feel when they encounter hypocrisy—and serves as a motivation for me to avoid it at all costs. There is, after all, nothing more revolting than telling people about Jesus but not living like him.

Frankly, I'm also glad that I was found out. Even though it hurt, it ended up being beneficial to my soul. Once I got over the embarrassment and anger, I was humbled. I ended up apologizing to Shelley. I told her that I really wanted to be a good Christian, and to be consistent with what said I believed, but that I was definitely still a work in progress. We understood each better after that; and even after we broke up several months later, we remained friends.

I hadn't come clean on my own. God had forced the issue. But I'm glad he did. When things are out in the open, they can be dealt with. That's when good things happen.

Listen, I understand that there is a huge difference between actual hypocrisy and simply being, well, human. We are going to make bad choices. We are going to possess "besetting sins," those flaws in our character that—try as we might—often get the best of us. We are going to fail to live up the standards God has set for us. Again, we are broken humans in need of redemption. "All have sinned and fallen short of the glory of God" (Romans 3:23).

But if we have any hope of successfully pursuing our God-given potential and becoming who he meant us to be, we have to take our own integrity seriously.

About the age I was making out with Shelley, I was also helping my dad install big organs at churches across Kansas. Organs are huge instruments, about 500–700 pounds, and when you load them up in a moving truck with all the speakers, dollies, and installation equipment, the combined mass weighs about a half a ton.

The first time I drove a Ryder truck to an install job, I noticed that not only was the truck significantly slowed down by the added weight, but the vehicle itself had what was called a "governor," a safety device that limited how fast I could drive. Even when I floored the gas, I could never get the speed over fifty-five miles per hour! I just puttered along in that big, lumbering beast. The truck handled like a barge, and it took forever to get anywhere. It was so frustrating.

But there was a fun part at the end. Once I'd returned the truck, I'd hop back into my mom's 1991 Hyundai Excel. It was a bright-red, quick little car, and the experience of driving it after the Ryder truck was like night and day. Suddenly, I felt like I was driving an Indy race car, racing down main-street

Hutchinson at Mach 3, taking corners like I was turning on a dime.

That's the difference between living a guilt-loaded, lumbering life with an uneasy conscience serving as "governor" and living fast and free, with a clear conscience.

After he sinned by committing adultery with Bathsheba, David struggled with physical symptoms of sin and guilt. He says in Psalm 32 that when he kept silent and did not confess his sin, his "bones wasted away" and he felt his guilt "heavy upon [him]" (Psalm 32:3–4). This, by the way, is consistent with what psychologists and counselors have discovered. Everyone except for the narcissists and sociopaths among us has a conscience. There is a universal sense of right and wrong possessed by the human race, and when a man or woman consistently lives contrary to that universal morality, their bodies manifest psychosomatic symptoms: weariness, brain fog, aches, "feeling blue," and even severe pains. Our bodies have a way of telling us when our souls are not in shape. We feel it physically when we are not healthy spiritually.

Proverbs 28:1 states, "The wicked flee when no one pursues them, but the righteous are bold as a lion." Translation: when you're a hypocrite, when you choose to live with inconsistency and unconfessed sin in your life, you're going to be burdened with fear and paranoia. It's going to affect everything you do.

On the other hand, if your conscience is clear—if you are not perfect but consistent, and do your best to live with integrity—you will be "bold as a lion." You will be able to live with real confidence and power. Liberated from the burden of guilt and an uneasy conscience, you'll be happy and at peace. That happiness will provide the energy to pursue your God-given potential, to go hard after your goals and dreams with enthusiasm. That peace will keep you calm in the midst of challenges and adversity.

Integrity is essential to your health—spiritually, emotionally, mentally, and physically. That's why one of the most important things you can do to continue to successfully pursue your God-given potential in life is . . .

. . . confess your sins.

There's a debate between Protestants and Catholics as to whether or not you "need" to confess your sins to a priest. I'm not going to get into that debate here. For now, I'll just say, if you're Protestant, think seriously about 1 John 1:9 and James 5:16. God is eager to forgive us, and there's power in opening up to a trusted brother or sister in Christ and identifying the areas in which you struggle.

If you're a Catholic with a personal relationship with Jesus (like I am), don't neglect the sacrament of confession. It is an unparalleled gift of grace that helps us put our sins behind us, "get back on the horse," and start living in faith, hope, and love again. Personally, I am always moved when I hear my spiritual director, Father Ryan McCandless, say "Go in peace. The Lord has freed you from your sins." I leave the confessional and walk out of church with a renewed energy and enthusiasm for life.

I've just unburdened my soul. Now I'm ready to pursue my potential and crush my goals—for my gain, the good of the world, and the glory of God!

That's how it works.

Take your integrity seriously. Examine your conscience. Confess your hypocrisy and all the ways you have fallen short of God's glory—not to beat yourself up, but to become who God made you to be. It feels so good to be liberated from guilt and energized by forgiveness.

That's a surprising connection between faith and fulfilling our potential, between spiritual virtue and becoming a peak performer. Living with integrity helps us live with intensity. Confession helps us crush.

QUESTIONS FOR REFLECTION

• Is there a flaw in your character that you have become comfortable with? A "besetting sin" that you have simply accepted as part of who you are? Considering that Jesus said "If your eye causes you to sin, tear it out," what radical thing do you need to do in order to finally deal with this crap in your soul?

• When was the last time you confessed your sin and felt the joy of God's gracious forgiveness? If you are Protestant, would you consider sharing a struggle with a trusted friend? If you are Catholic, would you commit to going to confession this week?

RECOMMENDED RESOURCES:

• Psalm 51 (David confesses to God after sinning with Bathsheba)

- John Wesley's Spiritual Discipline Self-Examination (22 Questions)

- *The Good and Beautiful Life: Putting On the Character of Christ* by James Bryan Smith

- *Lord, Have Mercy: The Healing Power of Confession* by Scott Hahn

Chapter Eleven

SAY "YES, SIR"

"Whenever, wherever, however You want me, I'll go. And I'll begin this very minute. Lord, as I stand up from this place, and as I take my first step forward, will You consider this is a step toward complete obedience to You? I'll call it the step of yes." **—Brother Andrew**

"Obedience is a consecration of the heart, chastity of the body, and poverty of all worldly goods to the Love and Service of God. Blessed indeed are the obedient, for God will never permit them to go astray." **—Saint Francis de Sales**

"He is no fool who gives what he cannot keep to gain what he cannot lose." **—Jim Elliot**

During my first stint of living in Manhattan, Kansas (2002–2011), I followed the career of an exceedingly talented farm boy who played quarterback for nearby Riley County High School. The first time I watched him play, I labeled him an underachiever. Sure, he was like a ballerina when he dropped back in the pocket, quick as lightning when he scrambled, and accurate as Robin Hood when he passed. But was he putting in maximum effort? It certainly didn't seem like it. In fact, it looked as if he were barely trying.

But I was wrong. What I thought was half-assed effort was really all-star athleticism. He was the proverbial "man among boys," a physical specimen as far superior to others on the field as a John Deere tractor is to hand-pushed single-row plows. He made it look easy, but judging him for his easy domination would be like criticizing an iPhone for the seemingly effortless way it sends texts to and from space. It doesn't mean it's not working hard.

Not surprisingly, this young man was recruited to play football for the hometown team, the Kansas State University Wildcats. The fan base *was* startled, however, when he wasn't recruited to play quarterback. Initially, he was tabbed to fill the defensive back position. But after his red-shirt year, he was invited to the office of Hall of Fame coach Bill Snyder; there, Coach Snyder told him that he was switching his position yet again, this time to wide receiver.

Now, never mind that the young man had never played wide receiver in his life—not in middle school, high school, or college—and that he had never run a route or caught a pass at any time during a game. When Bill Snyder told this young farm boy the position he was to play, the farm boy—according to an article later published in the *Milwaukee Journal Sentinel*—gave his coach a simple, two-word answer:

"*Yes, sir.*"

If there were any naysayers (and I'm sure there were), any who questioned Coach Snyder's judgment, they were quickly and decisively silenced. The young man's junior season playing wide receiver in the Big 12 conference was solid. His senior season was record-breaking. He earned all-conference and all-American honors. Upon graduating, he was drafted by the Green Bay Packers and immediately made an impact on the field. In 2011, the young man—who, if you haven't guessed yet, was *Jordy Nelson*—played a pivotal role in helping Gang Green win Super Bowl XLV.

Good thing he said, "Yes, sir," right?

As usual, hindsight is twenty-twenty. But things could have gone a very different direction. If you think about it, Jordy Nelson would have been justified in protesting his coach's decision. Who was to say he would excel in this new position? Would he adjust well? Or would the transition prove disastrous and ruin his chances of playing in the NFL? He could have said, "I'm on the team. I work hard. I want to win. I've only ever played quarterback. Why do I have to switch positions?"

Instead, at a critical moment in his career and life, he chose to believe that Bill Snyder knew what he was doing. He trusted him. He recognized the wisdom and experience of his Hall of Fame coach and submitted to his authority.

He said "Yes, sir."

Those two words communicated a powerful sentiment: *I know it's not enough to be on the team, to play hard, and to want to win. My coach gets to determine my position and call the plays.* And as a result, good things happened.

In Luke 4:1–13, we find the gospel account of Satan's temptation of Jesus. According to the Scriptures, Jesus was "led by the spirit for forty days, being tempted by the devil" (4:1–2). During that time, he ate nothing, and I think it's safe to say sleeping in the wilderness for more than a month had to be punishing on his body. The Bible clearly states that Jesus was hungry. Common sense tells us that he was sore and tired.

It's not uncommon for intelligence organizations like the

CIA to use sleep deprivation and acute exhaustion to induce spies and terrorists to cave under interrogation. When human beings are famished and frazzled, they are vulnerable to manipulation.

This was Satan's hope. A tired Savior could be tempted to turn away from the will of God. The devil's strategy was to twist Jesus's desire to honor his heavenly Father. He wanted to convince Jesus *that being the Son of God carried with it certain* privileges—and the exercise of those privileges was well within his rights.

"If you are the Son of God," Satan said, "command these stones to become bread."

The Son of God has the right to a full stomach!

"To you I will give all the kingdoms of the world and their glory," Satan promised, "if you just worship me."

The Son of God has the right to all the wealth and political power in the world!

"If you are the Son of God, throw yourself from the temple," Satan said. "Because your angels are going to catch you!"

The Son of God ought to do something sensational—so that he gains everyone's attention! (Satan would fit in really well with today's marketers.)

I encourage you to read the whole account of Jesus's temptation in the Gospel of Luke, but let's summarize this way: Every time Satan tempted Jesus, our Lord responded with a Scripture passage *that reasserted the will of God.*

Jesus did not question the truth of Satan's assumptions.

That is, it is absolutely true that the Son of God deserves all the best food (and drink) that this world has to offer.

It is true that the Son of God is entitled to all the political power and influence in the world. It is rightly his!

It is true that the Son of God should be renowned over all the earth—and that everyone's attention should be firmly fixed on him.

Satan was right. All these things were well within Jesus's rights.

But our Lord did not live according to his rights. He lived according to his responsibilities . . .

. . . and he knew that his responsibility was to follow—*to the letter*—God's plan for his life.

That plan involved self-denial.

It involved humility.

It involved suffering and dying on the cross.

Had Jesus embraced his rights, everything in this world would have gone wrong.

Instead, if I could be the first person in the history of the planet to draw an analogy between the King of Kings and a K-State football player, Jesus said:

"I know it's not enough to be on the team, to play hard, and to want to win. My coach gets to determine my position and call the plays."

The Carpenter from Nazareth who is the great lover of our souls said, "It's not enough that I am the Son of God. I must be the Son of God in exactly the way that my Father wants me to be and follow his plan for me, no matter the cost or sacrifice. I recognize his authority. I trust him. I know he wants the best for me."

For the record, this was not easy for Jesus. Though he was

without sin, he was fully human—just like us. So the prospect of hanging on a Roman cross and bearing the sins of the world was daunting to him. In fact, as he prayed in the Garden of Gethsemane the night before he was crucified, the Scriptures say he was in such anguish that he "sweat drops of blood" (Luke 22:44).

As he prayed in the garden, Our Lord knew that as he hung on the cross, he would not just experience excruciating physical pain. He would experience the far greater torture of taking our sin upon himself and, for the sake of our redemption, being forsaken by God. Enduring the curse that we ourselves earned.

> But he was pierced for our transgressions;
> he was crushed for our iniquities;
> upon him was the chastisement that brought us peace,
> nd with his wounds we are healed.
>
> (Isaiah 53:5)

> For our sake he made him to be sin who knew no sin, so that in him we might become the righteousness of God.
> (2 Corinthians 5:21)

Can you imagine the prospect of shouldering humanity's sin and being shut out from our Father's loving presence? No wonder Jesus said, "My soul is overwhelmed to the point of death!" (Matthew 26:28).

That is why it is incredibly understandable that Jesus asked if there were any other way: "Father, if you are willing, take this cup from me" (Luke 22:42).

And yet he followed up that question with a firm declaration: "Yet not mine, *but thy will be done.*" Facing the most overwhelming sorrow imaginable, Jesus Christ galvanized his will and resolved to move ahead.

To put it simply, he said, *"Yes, sir."*

Thank God he did.

"Dying he destroyed our death, rising he restored our life."

All of us can have peace with God and each other—hope, joy, and a future, both in this life and the life to come . . .

. . . because Jesus said, "Yes, sir."

The servant is not greater than the master.

If you desire to be a hard-driving kind of person—to be someone who is fierce, faithful, and fearless—you must respond to God's call on your life with an unqualified "Yes, sir."

You must go all in on obedience to him, with no compromise and no deviation.

As I will explain later in this book, this does not mean that we have no freedom to chart a path for our lives or live out our faith in a way that is unique to us. It does mean that, when all is said and done, you must recognize that it is God's right to determine the context of his calling on your life. He has the right to determine your position and call the plays. Your job is to accept your role and play hard, trusting that God knows exactly what he is doing and that he has your best interests in mind.

I want to tell you—from personal experience—that our coach does know what he is doing. He does have our best interest in mind. Twenty-five years ago, if you asked me what my future held, I would have told you I was going to be an evangelical pastor and preacher. Today, I'm a Catholic writer, speaker, and podcaster and the director of development for St. Isidore's Catholic Student Center in Manhattan, Kansas (the best college town in the nation, by the way).

That old saying is true: "If you want to hear God laugh, tell him your plans." But something else is true: when you discover his plans for you, you'll laugh too—because you'll realize how absurd you were for thinking you had a better plan for experiencing God's best for your life.

My life has been an adventure I never imagined. To recap what I told you in the introduction to this book (just in case you skipped it): Over the last couple years, I've cohosted a podcast that earned millions of downloads each month. I've been privileged to meet amazing people—everyone from Tim Grover (Michael Jordan and Kobe Bryant's personal trainer) to Lou Holtz (the former college football coach who won the national championship with Notre Dame). Through the influence of my former boss Andy Frisella, his brother Sal, and their company 1st Phorm (best fitness supplements in the business!), I've learned how to raise my standards of excellence, productivity, and mental toughness.

As a result, I have learned what it means not just to be faithful but to be fierce and fearless. The book you are reading right now would not have been written if I had insisted on playing the position I wanted to play, rather than listening to my coach. Thankfully, by God's grace, I was able to say "Yes, sir"—and my life has unfolded, not without heartache and hardship, but "immeasurably more than I could ever have asked or imagined" (Ephesians 3:20).

When you say "Yes, sir" to God, that firm reliance on him and total abandonment to his will translate into a confidence that everything will work out as it was meant to be. The negativity of fear and doubt will give way to a positive, faith-driven optimism that truly believes that "nothing is impossible with God" (Luke 1:37).

Let God determine your position and call the plays in your life, no matter what. Embrace the mindset that always says "yes," to him, and he'll empower you with his spirit. He will enable you to pursue your God-given potential with a holy ferocity, with faith, and without fear.

QUESTIONS FOR REFLECTION

• Where did you see yourself ending up five, ten, twenty years ago? Is your life in the present moment different from how you thought it would turn out? What unexpected paths have ultimately made you better?

• Think about an area in your life where you've clung onto control because you think you deserve it. Is it holding you back from other opportunities?

• Take some time to evaluate the different aspects of your life. Is there an area where you are clearly not saying, "Yes, sir!" to God?

RECOMMENDED RESOURCES

• *An Introduction to the Devout Life* by St. Francis de Sales

• *The Cost of Discipleship* by Dietrich Bonhoeffer

Chapter Twelve

ACCEPT GIFTS, ELIMINATE IDOLS

"I have learned to hold all things loosely, so God will not have to pry them out of my hands." —**Corrie ten Boom**

"God gives me whatever I want, because I want whatever He gives." —**Saint Therese of Lisieux**

I was certain that marrying Kasia was the right call.

As I stated in another chapter, the moment I met her felt like a mystical experience. Though I did not tell her at that moment, it seemed to me as if God had a special plan; not for me and her separately, but for the two of us *together*.

Early in our relationship, we were hiking together in the Konza Prairie when she asked, "Why did you go *twelve years* not dating anyone? Why did you decide, after all that time, to pursue *me*?"

Kasia knew that my last serious relationship had ended in 1997—that I had been dumped at the International House of Pancakes by a pastor's daughter that I was certain I was going to marry. (That, by the way, was more wishful thinking than any real clear-headed reflection on the matter.) It was a massive disappointment to me, which led me to struggle with discouragement, depression, and anger toward God. For a time,

I inwardly shook my fist at him; and though I never had the heart for a full-scale walk on the wild side, I secretly dabbled at "the rebellious life."

Eventually, I did meet several nice women and had opportunities to date. But I was just never interested enough to get serious, just never motivated enough to put in the effort needed to build the kind of deep relationship that could lead to "I now pronounce you man and wife."

If I was honest with myself, though, my lack of motivation was rooted in fear. I had high hopes for my previous relationship—and had been disappointed. I had put my heart and soul into loving that pastor's daughter—and had been rejected. I had dreamed big about our life together—and the dream had evaporated.

"I don't know," I answered Kasia. "It sounds cliché, but I think you are different. You want what I want.

"You want to live an epic life."

Kasia would later reveal to me that, in prayer, she often asked God to send her a husband who "wanted to live an epic life."

Although that is a cool detail in our story, the other thing I told her was absolutely true: she was different. There is a great verse in Song of Solomon—the Bible's book on romantic love—that describes how I felt about Kasia: "like a lily among thorns is my darling among the young women" (2:2). That's not to say I felt like other women were thorns! I just felt like Kasia was qualitatively distinct from other women I'd encountered. In my opinion, what made her so different was that she wasn't an either/or kind of woman. She was both/and.

The women I met were often *either* sweet, godly women

who had *no* other ambitions except becoming a wife and mother ...

... or they were hyper-independent, driven "career woman" who would rather close a deal than cuddle a child.

Kasia's dream was to marry a good man and raise a large family, and she cherished being a wife and mother above anything else. But at the same time, she had personal ambitions and aspirations: she was in medical school, training to become a family physician. She loved learning. She loved running and working out. She loved dreaming and setting goals for herself. She was—and is—committed to pursuing her God-given potential.

Other women I met were *either* morally virtuous *or* down-to-earth. They were devoutly religious, but they didn't seem to understand how to have fun. They knew how to be holy and blameless, but they didn't know how to be kind and gracious to those who struggled spiritually.

Or the opposite was true: they paid lip service to faith, but they were moral train wrecks. They knew how to party, but they knew nothing about prayer. They might have looked great at the beach, but they were shallow as a birdbath.

Kasia had real faith, real character, *and* she was a real, down-to-earth woman. Our relationship wasn't just built around our mutual faith in Christ. It worked because we could be real with each other. We could talk about our hopes and dreams, but we could also be vulnerable with each other: sharing our doubts, fears, and the darker parts of ourselves. Even though Kasia was—and is—a very virtuous woman, I never felt judged for my mistakes and sins.

Of course, Kasia also brought her own issues and baggage into our relationship. It didn't matter to me. By that time, I was old enough to know that no human being was perfect, no relationship was perfect, and no marriage was going to be anywhere near perfect. But I also knew that a marriage didn't have to be perfect to be *great*.

I was ready for a great marriage and a great life. We'd been dating for three years—getting engaged seemed like the logical next step to take the euphoria of love to the next level. I just knew that even deeper love awaited us on the other side of the altar.

However, where engagements are supposed to strengthen relationships, ours ended up having the opposite effect on Kasia. I'd expected it to make us even closer, but instead she grew more and more consumed by anxiety, constantly seeming as though she'd started to get cold feet.

Finally, one night she told me we had to have a serious discussion about whether our love really had what it took. The conclusion, at least for her? It didn't.

"I think we should break up," she said.

Part of me wanted to protest, to argue that she wasn't being rational. She had often struggled with some relationship fears that had been rooted in family-of-origin issues. I wanted to tell her that we could just work harder to address those fears, that they were making whatever weaknesses we had as a couple seem bigger and more serious than they actually were. Part of me wanted to convince her that she was just being a perfectionist, and that expecting perfection in a relationship was going to prevent her from actually enjoying and embracing it.

But a bigger part of me realized that actually . . . I agreed. Whether her concerns were reasonable or not, Kasia was miserable, and watching the engagement twist her into knots had made me miserable too. It just wasn't sustainable.

"Yes," I replied. "I think you're right."

Initially, I was in shock—the rest of the evening passed in a distant blur I still struggle to remember. Eventually, the numbness turned into a sharp ache, as though I'd been punched in the gut—hard. That night, as I climbed into bed and my sweet yellow lab Rudy nuzzled up next to me, the ache still hadn't gone away. I didn't feel that I had been rejected so much as simply left. I felt Kasia's presence recede from me, leaving the world a suddenly empty, lonely place. As I lay in bed, I didn't fall asleep—it simply got darker and darker until I was no longer awake.

* * *

As I woke up, rays of sunlight fell on my face through my bedroom window, bathing me in a gentle warmth. Rudy, who had rested his head on my knees to comfort me just eight hours earlier, was curled up in a toasty ball at the foot of my bed; sensing my return from slumber, he started wagging his tail.

I sat up, swiveled, and stepped onto the wood floor, stretching in the morning sunshine. Wiping my eyes, I took a couple deep breaths, and then wondered, *What's that I feel?*

I'd expected the previous night's hollowness to linger like a phantom pain, crashing down on me as soon as I remembered I was single. I should have felt discouraged. Depressed. Heartbroken.

But without even looking in a mirror, I could tell I was . . . smiling.

I felt peace. Hopeful anticipation.

Joy!

I felt *great.*

What the hell is going on? I thought. *Am I in denial? Is this some sort of knee-jerk Strong-Christians-Can't-Grieve-or-Question-God response?*

No.

What I felt wasn't a façade. I wasn't just pasting a smiley face on a soul in turmoil.

What I felt was real. The joy I was experiencing was true and good and beautiful.

So how could I explain it?

In the absence of an answer, I shrugged and turned to my dog. "Rudy," I said. "Let's go for a run!"

After quickly pulling on some clothes and my running shoes, I clipped on my iPod, put in my earphones, and cued up the soundtrack from *Rocky IV*!

As I ran through the streets of Atchison, Kansas (where I lived at the time) and down by the riverfront, I moved harder and happier than I had in a long, long time, losing myself to the wave of excitement and enthusiasm that washed over me. Even as endorphins surged through me, though, still I wondered, *Why do I feel so good?*

After my run, I stopped by the adoration chapel at St. Benedict's Church and started to pray for a few moments. As

I prayed, I believe the Holy Spirit prompted me to remember a conversation I'd had with Kasia when we first started dating.

We'd been hanging out at Scooter's Coffee in Kansas City. Somehow, the conversation had turned to past relationships, and I'd told Kasia I'd learned something really valuable when a previous relationship fell apart. "I learned that you can never make someone you love into an idol. They always have to be accepted as a gift from God."

"I like thinking of relationships as gifts," Kasia said. "Saint John Paul the Great talks about the Law of the Gift. He said that love is 'a total gift of yourself to the other person.'"

She took a sip of her drink.

"This German-chocolate-cake latte is a gift!" she said.

I chuckled.

"What does that really mean, practically?" she asked. "I mean, accepting someone as a gift?"

"When my old girlfriend and I broke up," I'd replied, "I went into a bad funk. I got bitter. Angry with God. And the ways I expressed that anger weren't honoring to him. After a while, I realized I'd made an idol out of Stephanie. An idol is a false god. It's *something other than God* that you try to find your ultimate happiness in. Mine turned me into an addict. I was thinking, *If I can't have Stephanie in my life, I can't be happy.*"

To her credit, rather than rolling her eyes at my waxing philosophical, Kasia at least pretended to take me seriously. "You don't think the person you love should make you happy?"

"Sure! But the best way for you to make me happy is for me to think of you as a gift from God. You're a gift that's valuable. A gift that really does make me happy. But at the end of the day, you're a gift that can never replace the Giver of All Good Things."

Recalling that conversation, I suddenly realized why I felt so good. On that day three years earlier, I had told Kasia—I'd actually promised her—that no matter what happened between us, I would never let her become an idol in my life. If we ended up getting married, I would be incredibly happy. But if she ended up walking away, while I might be sad, I'd never again let myself be overcome by sinister bitterness.

I truly believe that the joy I felt the day after our breakup was the Holy Spirit filling my heart with peace and confidence, because I hadn't let Kasia become an idol. I had embraced her as a gift—and even after a broken engagement, a "gift" is what she remained.

At that moment in the Adoration Chapel, I started getting really, really excited. That's when I felt God whisper to me.

Well, Vaughn. What do you want to do now?

I didn't hesitate.

"I don't need Kasia to be happy, Lord," I said. "But I love her. And I want her in my life!"

I heard the Lord whisper again. *So what do you want to do?*

I crossed myself, stood up, walked out of the Adoration Chapel, and said out loud . . .

"I want to marry Kasia Szymanek. So I'm going to do everything I can to win her back!"

That's when God whispered, *Go for it.*[2]

---

2 In case you skipped ahead to this chapter . . . yes, I fought hard for Kasia's love, came up with a pretty brilliant plan to woo her . . . and I won her back. A year later, we were married. ;)

I tell you that story because all of us have things in our lives that we really, really want. Those things could be:

- material possessions, like a car or a house

- a dream job, in your chosen field or with a high salary

- an opportunity, like playing football for a college or NFL team

- an accomplishment, like being elected governor or even president

- a relationship, like a husband or wife

I truly believe that none of those things, in and of themselves, are bad. They can be—and often are—gifts that God gives his faithful ones, and many are the natural result of being good stewards of our lives. Someone who conducts their life with integrity, vision, hard work, and kindness will often have doors of opportunity open to them, and many of those opportunities come with financial and material benefits.

But this isn't always the case. Sometimes God doesn't bless our efforts. He doesn't always allow our plans to work out the way we wanted. Often, for reasons known only to him, he allows us to experience loss, calamity, and disappointment. In the real world, people who love God can still suffer from financial troubles, rebellious children, bad health, or a wayward spouse.

In that coffee-shop talk with Kasia, I explained that there's a huge difference between making someone an idol and accepting them into your life as a gift. When you regard that person as an idol, you're saying, "I need them. Without them, I cannot be happy." But when you regard them as a gift, you're saying, "I want this person in my life, and I want to experience happiness with them. I am so glad God put them in my life—but if he chooses to take them away, while I may grieve, I will not rebel. Above all, I will be thankful—and I will remain faithful. 'The Lord gives and the Lord takes away. Blessed be the name of the Lord'" (Job 1:21).

In moments of loss, we need to ask ourselves whether we regard all good things in our lives as idols or as gifts. Do we need them to be happy? Is our faithfulness contingent on whether we possess them or not? Or do we simply value and enjoy them, accepting them as a gift from the hand of the Giver, the only real source of happiness each of us can ever truly rely on?

When God asked his servant Abraham to sacrifice his son, Isaac (Genesis 22), Abraham was old. He had waited *years* for the blessing of his son, and God had promised that he would become a great nation through his offspring. People who first hear this story are often shocked that God would ask such a thing. It's important to note that he didn't let Abraham go through with the sacrifice—Isaac was spared. But God needed to test Abraham, to see if Abraham placed God highest no matter what—or if his faith and obedience were contingent on possessing Isaac, his beloved son.

They weren't. Through incredible faith, Abraham demonstrated to God that no gift—no matter how precious—was greater to him than the Giver. As a result, God blessed Abraham, and he became the father of the great nation of

Israel. Through Israel came the Savior, Jesus Christ. And even though God allowed Abraham to spare his son, God himself did not spare his only Son, Jesus, but gave him up for us all, that we might be saved.

In the New Testament, Jesus opens his Sermon on the Mount with the words, "Blessed are the poor in spirit, for theirs is the kingdom of God" (5:3). It's interesting that in the Gospel of Luke, it just says, "Blessed are the poor" (Luke 6:20). Poor people are those who possess nothing. When you are "poor in spirit," it means that you don't *insist* on possessing anything. Rather than demanding what you want of God, you gratefully accept his gifts into your life, and freely submit when those gifts are removed. When Jesus says, "If anyone would come after me, let him deny himself, take up his cross, and follow me" (Matthew 16:24), he is speaking about this attitude—the attitude that says, "When I follow Jesus, I don't need anything." As my favorite saint, Saint Philip Neri, says, "He who wishes for anything but Christ, does not know what he wishes; he who asks for anything but Christ, does not know what he is asking; he who works, and not for Christ, does not know what he is doing."

In a phrase, we are to be delightfully detached. We can be driven to pursue excellence in our lives, and we can be delighted if God gives us the opportunity to experience certain gifts—a sports car, a nice house, a position as president of a college, or a beloved spouse. But even if we never get those things, or they are taken away from us, that's okay. We never needed them in the first place. All we needed—and ultimately, all we wanted—was the Giver, God himself.

A. W. Tozer said it best in his classic book, *The Pursuit of God*:

> There can be no doubt that clinging to things is one of the most harmful habits in life. Because it's so natural, it's rarely recognized for the evil that it is, but its outworkings are tragic. We are often hindered from giving up our treasures to the Lord out of fear for their safety; this is especially true when those treasures are loved relatives and friends. But we need have no such fears. Our Lord came not to destroy but to save. Everything is safe which we commit to him, and nothing is really safe which is not so committed.

Do you understand the peace and the power that are possessed by someone who is not possessed by a need for anything but God?

That person cannot be bought. Because their happiness is not contingent on material possessions.

That person cannot be bullied. Because their happiness is not contingent on their social status or connections.

That person is free from all the influences that daily intimidate and entangle the average human being.

They are liberated from the fear of losing anything, because they know that they can never really lose the one thing that makes them happy: God's presence in their lives.

There is no better way to pursue your God-given potential and become exceptional than to always accept good things into your life as gifts, not try to possess them as idols.

All things must be committed to him for us to become truly exceptional. No exceptions.

QUESTIONS FOR REFLECTION

• Have you allowed a good gift in your life to become an idol? Has it replaced God as the main source of happiness in your life? Take time to ask God to remove that idol from your heart and take his rightful place at center of your soul.

• Has God recently taken a good gift away from you? How have you responded? Are you sorrowful but still faithful? Or are you descending into bitterness and resentment, clinging to a gift instead of the Giver? Confess your idolatry to God, ask him to heal your anger, and ask him to fill you with a sense of peace and trust in his will.

RECOMMENDED RESOURCES

• "The Blessedness of Possessing Nothing" (chapter in *The Pursuit of God* by A. W. Tozer)

• *Avoiding Bitterness in Suffering: How Our Heroes in Faith Found Peace Amid Sorrow* by Dr. Ronda Chervin

Chapter Thirteen

DO YOU (AMDG)

"For as in one body we have many members, and the members do not all have the same function, so we, though many, are one body in Christ, and individually members one of another." —**Romans 12:4-5**

"Find out who you are and do it on purpose." —**Dolly Parton**

When I was a student at Wheaton College, I idolized A. W. Tozer, a Protestant pastor and writer who made a powerful impact on my life through books such as *The Knowledge of the Holy* and *The Pursuit of God*. Tozer lived and died before my time, but since he had served a small church in the Chicago area, less than an hour from where I went to school, I was able to arrange a meeting with Harry Verploegh, an elder in Tozer's church who'd known him personally. I felt like I was meeting a direct link to one of the original apostles!

A gracious old man by that time, Harry was impressive and delightful. His words were both winsome and wise: he recounted the many ways that Tozer glorified God during his daily life, the concrete examples of Christian character he provided, and the deep insights he possessed about knowing and loving God. I was transfixed. But then Harry changed the direction of the conversation:

"You know, Vaughn," he said. "Tozer was a great Christian

man. C. S. Lewis was a great Christian man. Augustine was a great saint. But you can't be Tozer or Lewis or Augustine."

That gave me pause. What did he mean?

"You have to be you. If you won't be yourself, nobody can do it for you. And so the Church and the world will be without your unique contribution."

That meant a lot to me.

It's great to want to be like our favorite saint or godly person—we should strive to imitate their faith, hope, and love.

But that desire for imitation can be twisted by the devil and our weak conscience into a tendency to compare ourselves to others, which has profoundly negative consequences. When we compare ourselves, that leads to guilt, confusion, and ultimately discouragement.

- Guilt
  - "Why can't I love books and studying as much as Saint Thomas Aquinas loved them?"
    - God may have given you a completely different personality than Saint Thomas. Perhaps he wired you to feel most alive when you are gazing at a sunset or serving at a soup kitchen.

- Confusion
  - "I admire Saint Teresa of Calcutta so much, and she dedicated herself to the poor. Do I have to do that?"
  - "So many of my friends are going into overseas missions. Is it bad that I have no desire to do that?"

- You can admire someone's faith and not follow in their exact footsteps. A noble calling
  for others may not be the calling God has de-
  signed for you.

- Discouragement
  - "Why am I not happy as a Christian? Why is the exer-
    cise of my faith so burdensome to me?"
    - It may be that you are trying to live out your
      faith and life as someone other than yourself,
      someone you think others want you to be
      rather than who God actually made you.

Guilt, confusion, and discouragement undermine our ability to be fierce, faithful, and fearless. If we are going to be
hard-driving souls who never give up in the pursuit of their
God-given potential, *we need to understand just who it is God
calls us to be.*

Remember: in relating to other believers, all we are called
to "copy" is their commitment to Christ. Whatever virtues
they possess are ones we should pursue. That's what Saint
Paul meant when he wrote, "Join in imitating me, and keep
your eyes on those who walk according to the example you
have in us" (Philippians 3:17). Beyond that, we are given the
freedom to express ourselves, to pursue the life that is best
suited to our God-given personality, temperament, interests,
and skills.

In his book *Philip Neri: The Fire of Joy*, Paul Türks describes the Oratory of Saint Philip Neri, which is the spiritual community that was inspired by his life and faith. He writes:

> The Spirit of the Oratory consists in this: letting each one find his own place, laying no compulsion on anyone, allowing each within the necessary limits to express in the individuality of his thought and his personality and rejoicing in the diversity as well as in the unity, having infinite respect for the individuality of each of one's [brothers and sisters in Christ]. *It is the freedom of the children of God. It is the true freedom that can only exist where the Spirit of the Lord is* [emphasis mine].[3]

That last phrase is key.

When you dedicate yourself to the glory of God and commit yourself to his will, there is infinite freedom to be yourself!

Think of it this way: the song "Over the Rainbow," originally recorded by Judy Garland for *The Wizard of Oz*, is one of the most covered songs in history. In addition to its innumerable renditions on *American Idol*, it's been sung by everyone from Willie Nelson and Eric Clapton to Tori Amos and Me First & The Gimme Gimmes.

Obviously, Judy Garland set the standard. Her performance is the first one people ever heard, and it's still the one the majority associate with the song. But so many of the covers are equally iconic! You know what that means? It means that people don't mind one great song sung by many different

---

3 Page 126

people. Actually, it means that people want a great song to be sung . . .

. . . in a different voice . . .

. . . in a different style . . .

. . . in a different arrangement . . .

. . . each rendition revealing a unique facet of the song that was just waiting to be uncovered.

In the same way, there is one universal "song" we are all called to perform: the song that gives glory to God and offers good to the world. But the key in which we sing that song, the notes which we choose to arrange it, and the style in which we choose to play it are utterly unique.

We have the freedom—actually, the responsibility—to perform it as only we can.

Not only does God want us to be ourselves, but to fulfill his calling in our lives, we must be ourselves.

Not only can I not be Tozer or Lewis or Augustine, *I shouldn't try to be.* This would be a detriment to my personal development and my quest for a God-honoring life. The Holy Spirit wants to guide me, and the love of God captivate me, *as God has uniquely made me.*

I cannot be an exact copy of someone else—even a saint or extremely holy person—and be the best version of myself. The person who is my ultimate role model, Jesus Christ, will— and *should*—look different in my life than he does in someone else's.

This is not just allowed; it is essential.

The Church is the Body of Christ, and the fullness of that

Body is beautifully expressed in the richness and diversity of each individual member (1 Corinthians 12:12–27).

Again, as Harry Verploegh said, "If you won't be you, no one can be you for you; and the Church and the world will be without your unique contribution."

With this in mind, we ought to be relentless about understanding who God made us to be. The ancient Oracle at Delphi said that the key to wisdom is to "know thyself." That is true, but it's important to note that we aren't pursuing self-knowledge to be self-obsessed. Quite the opposite. We are looking inward so that we can live upwardly and outwardly. Our knowledge of ourselves is meant to translate into love of God and service to others.

So, as I like to say, "mine what's yours." In other words, begin to take an inventory of what is uniquely you. Spend time thinking about what you offer the world. Get alone and think about it. Journal. Freewrite. Take advantage of personality tests and spiritual gift inventories. Here are some things to consider:

- Pleasures – What brings you joy?

- Pain – What suffering have you endured?

- Places – Where have you lived? How have they shaped you?

- People – Who has most influenced you in your life?

- Privileges – What have you enjoyed that others haven't? Education? Travel?

- "Powers" – What are you good at? Talents?

- Proclivities – What are you interested in?

Get to know yourself. What kind of person did God make you, and what can you offer the world?

Ralph Waldo Emerson once said, "To be yourself in a world that is constantly trying to make you something else is the greatest accomplishment."

I would tweak that statement to read "To be *who God made you to be* in a world that is constantly trying to make you something else is a *great act of worship*."

All this to say:

Do everything *ad majorem Dei gloriam*[4] (for the greater glory of God)! ...

... and do good in the world.

As only you can do it.

QUESTIONS FOR REFLECTION

- Frederick Buechner once wrote, "The place God calls you is where your deep gladness and the world's deep hunger meet." Personally, what brings you great happiness? Is there a way you can pursue that happiness that helps solve a problem or meet a need in today's world? That may be the calling that is uniquely suited to you. Spend time journaling and praying about that this week.

- In what ways are you unfairly comparing yourself to other Christians in a way that produces guilt, confusion, and discouragement? Take time to identify this and ask God to liberate you to love him and be yourself.

---

4 Or as the cool kids like to put it, "AMDG"

• Do you understand the difference between choosing a saint or holy person to be a role model and feeling the compulsion to be exactly like them? Identify two or three godly men and women (in heaven or still on earth) you want to imitate (not replicate!). Take time to reflect on the virtues they possess that you want to pursue. But also take the time to identify how you are unique from them and how you will do things differently in your own life.

RECOMMENDED RESOURCES:

• *Sacred Pathways: Discover Your Soul's Path to God* by Gary Thomas

• *Perfectly Yourself: Discovering God's Dream for You* by Matthew Kelly

• *Type A Christian: Transforming Personality Traits into Fruitful Growth* by Autumn Hoover

Chapter Fourteen

VALUE YOUR BODY

"Or do you not know that your body is a temple of the Holy Spirit within you, whom you have from God? You are not your own, for you were bought with a price. So glorify God in your body." **—Saint Paul, First Epistle to the Corinthians**

"This is flesh I'm talking about here. Flesh that needs to be loved. Feet that need to rest and to dance; backs that need support; shoulders that need arms, strong arms I'm telling you."**—Toni Morrison, *Beloved***

When Kasia and I were still dating, she noticed a few odd things about my behavior—and thought she had a scientific explanation for them.

She noticed that (1) I would often space out, which for the longest time she interpreted as me becoming withdrawn and emotionally unavailable; (2) I would periodically go into "mini-funks," bouts of deep depression that generally only lasted three to four days, which made her believe that I had some kind of depressive disorder; (3) I would often complain of having "brain fog," barely able to string two lucid sentences together, which she attributed to internalized stress; and (4) I would get tired and worn out much more easily than a man of my health and fitness should, making her wonder, *What on earth is wrong with my boyfriend?*

Eventually, she rejected all the psychological, emotional,

and even spiritual explanations for why I struggled with those things. No, in her mind, she knew exactly what the problem was. It was actually very simple.

"I think you have food allergies."

Food allergies? I thought. *I've never had food allergies!* Besides, how could what you eat cause all those problems?

Did I mention my girlfriend (soon-to-be wife) was a doctor?

"Of *course* it could cause those problems," she said. "Allergy sensitivities cause inflammation. Inflammation can cause everything from brain fog and sluggishness to feeling depressed and emotionally strung out."

Didn't matter that I wasn't a doctor. I wasn't buying it.

"Listen," I said. "It's just the way I'm wired. I'm prone to what some early Christians called 'debilitating melancholy.' That means I'm just a sensitive soul. Those things are probably the result of sin in my life, or demonic attack, or something like that. Or maybe I have some trauma from childhood that I've buried and haven't dealt with yet, and that's what's causing it."

Now, as Kasia and I talked, we did agree that emotional issues and psychosomatic symptoms like fatigue and depression can have a spiritual source. But she was pretty emphatic that a significant amount of my symptoms could be attributed to a simple explanation: I was eating things I shouldn't be eating.

I resisted her. I refused to go off wheat and dairy, as she suggested. What! No cream in my coffee? No Minsky's deep-dish pepperoni pizza with extra cheese? No Wildcat burger from Kite's Bar and Grill? Impossible!

It wasn't until a year or so after Kasia and I got married,

SACRED DRIVE

when I went to hang out with my friend Barret, that I decided it might be legit. I told Barret about what I thought was her ludicrous theory, and was surprised by his response.

"Kasia thinks I need to go off gluten and dairy," I lamented to Barret. "She thinks my weird symptoms have to do with food allergies."

"Oh, totally, dude!" Barret said. "That's a thing. For sure. I know this girl who went off gluten, lost sixty pounds, and felt a billion times better."

"Really?" I said. "Okay, cool. I'll do it!"

That was that.

"You don't listen to your doctor wife," Kasia later told me, rolling her eyes. "But you listened to your college-age friend."

"Hey," I said. "He's my bro."

So I went off gluten and dairy. Guess what?

Within a couple weeks, I felt like a new man! My ability to concentrate was exponentially better. I had more energy. Sure, I still struggled with being down in the dumps from time to time, but that was usually because I had a rational reason to be discouraged. (Like I didn't feel like I was performing well at work. Or the political divisiveness of our nation got to me. Or they cast Ben Affleck as Batman.)

But at the end of the day, my mind felt clearer, my body felt better, and guess what? This positively affected my spiritual life.

What I'm trying to say is that, yes, you could be in spiritual turmoil because you're harboring sin against God in your heart. Or you could be in some sort spiritual warfare with the Forces of Darkness.

VAUGHN KOHLER

Or . . .

You could just be allergic to wheat or dairy.

You could have respiratory problems because there's mold in your house.

You could struggle with chronic fatigue syndrome because you have a genetic predisposition to it.

In other words, there could be a physical reason that you are struggling spiritually. Your soul may be suffering with your body.

If you want to pursue your God-given potential, what you need to fully understand—or at least remind yourself of again and again—is that there is a direct relationship between your body and your soul. The Catechism of the Catholic Church puts it nicely: "human beings are a unity of the physical and the spiritual." This statement is clearly supported in Scripture. The book of Genesis often relates historical events in mythopoetic language, using vivid literary imagery. To describe the creation of Adam, the first man, the Bible says that God created his body from the "dust of the ground" and breathed into him the "breath of life." The word we translate "breath" is the Hebrew *ruach*, which can also be translated "wind" or "spirit." This passage clearly communicates not only the two constituent parts of every human being—body and soul—but also their deep connectedness.

What is interesting is that, throughout the history of the Church, true believers have defended the importance of the body against the false and dangerous idea that the body doesn't matter, or even that it is bad. One of the earliest major heresies was Gnosticism, which taught that all physical matter, including our bodies (and Christ's body), was corrupted. They believed that only the spiritual could be pure, so they denied the redeeming power of the incarnation and Christ's physical resurrection, claiming that his appearances after Easter were merely a spiritual presence, that he had become "purified" through his death. This could not be further from the truth; Saint John wrote that "the Word [a title for Jesus] *became flesh* and dwelt among us" (John 1:14, emphasis mine), showing the powerful fact of the incarnation. Similarly, Saint Luke, in his gospel, really emphasizes the physicality of Jesus after his resurrection:

> And when he had said this, he showed them his hands and his feet. And while they still disbelieved for joy and were marveling, he said to them, 'Have you anything here to eat?' They gave him a piece of broiled fish, and he took it and ate before them.
>
> (Luke 24:40–42)

Saint Paul went so far as to say, "If Christ has not been raised, your faith is futile; you are still in your sins . . . [and] if the dead are not raised, 'Let us eat and drink, for tomorrow we die'" (1 Corinthians 15:14,32). In context, it is clear that the Apostle means raised physically; that is, literally and metaphorically. The renowned America novelist John Updike captured Paul's sentiments well:

"Make no mistake: if He rose at all it was as His body; if the cells' dissolution did not reverse, the molecules reknit, the amino acids rekindle, the Church will fall."[5]

---

5 "Seven Stanzas at Easter"

All this to say, from the resurrection to this day, Christianity has always emphasized the importance of our physical bodies.

When we sin sexually, we sin against our own bodies (1 Corinthians 6:18).

When our lives are evaluated at the Last Judgment, one of the most important criteria is whether we met the *physical* needs of the poor and hungry (James 2:16).

But bodies aren't just an occasion of sin for us, an opportunity to fall or fail to do justice for our brothers and sisters. Christianity has always taught that Christ, by entering creation, dignified it. That doesn't just include our bodies, it *especially means* our bodies. By becoming one of us, Jesus changed what "one of us" means, including "people with bodies." Contrary to popular belief, heaven is not a cloud-filled, disembodied state. Eternal life with Jesus means living in physical, resurrected bodies, like his own, in a physical universe that has been resurrected and restored to perfection (1 Corinthians 15).

In addition to all this, it is very telling (in my opinion) that three of the major metaphors for the Christian life involve physical training and exertion. Of all the ways he describes the life of faith, Saint Paul uses three analogies more than any other: Christians are like farmers, athletes, and soldiers (2 Timothy 2:3–6). Farming requires immense physical toil. Athletes must work hard to perfect their bodies for competition. Prior to the dawn of modern weaponry, soldiers could not possibly hope to win a battle unless they were in peak physical condition.

The implications for those of us who want to pursue our God-given potential are obvious: if we want to be all that God wants us to be, we must take our physical fitness seriously.

We must eat well, stay hydrated, exercise regularly, and get good rest and sleep. More than that, if we are serious about improving ourselves, evolving as human beings, we must challenge ourselves physically, just like we would challenge ourselves mentally and spiritually.

In other words, it is great for a believer to want to study hard to gain greater understanding of, say, the doctrine of the Trinity. It is obviously valuable for a Christian to want to challenge themselves to pray more often. But it is also valuable for a man or woman of God to commit to more difficult physical challenges: to graduate from running 5Ks, for example, to training for half marathons.

The reality is, too many Christians use Saint Paul's words as a proof text: "For physical training is of some value, but godliness has value in all things" (1 Timothy 4:8). Too many amateur Bible interpreters have read this to mean the Apostle is downplaying the importance of physical exercise. He's not. He's emphasizing the importance of godliness! But if you take the rest of the Bible into account, it is clear that fundamental to godliness is how you take care of and train your body. It is, after all, the "temple of the Holy Spirit." Wouldn't we want that temple to be built in the most sound, sturdy way, presented as beautifully as possible?

I can tell you from my own life that when I place value on my physical health and well-being, good things happen in my spiritual life. When I become more disciplined in the gym, that discipline overflows into my Bible reading and prayer life. When I learn to exercise, regardless of whether I feel like it or not, it conditions me to resist various temptations, whether I feel like doing what God desires of me or not. Training to become physically fit reminds me of the importance of training to become spiritually mature.

To be a Christian, both theologically and practically, is to recognize that our bodies matter, and what we do to and with them matters. If we genuinely believe that they are temples of the Holy Spirit, we are obliged to treat them with reverence and care, disciplining body and soul so that we can grow close to God, and eventually enjoy eternity with him.

QUESTIONS FOR REFLECTION

• Am I a good steward of the body God gave me? What areas (food, water, exercise, sleep) could I improve upon?

• How could I challenge myself to train harder, to improve myself physically?

RECOMMENDED RESOURCES

• 1stPhorm.com—Andy Frisella's company offers a wide variety of supplements to keep your body in peak condition, such as Level-1 protein supplement, Opti-Greens superfood powder, and Micro Factor complete daily nutrient packs.

• 75Hard—although not a "fitness challenge," the program will train you physically as you develop mental toughness

• *Eat Smarter: Use the Power of Food to Reboot Your Metabolism, Upgrade Your Brain, and Transform Your Life* and *Sleep Smarter: 21 Essential Strategies to Sleep Your Way to a Better Body, Better Health, and Bigger Success* by Shawn Stevenson

Chapter Fifteen

PURSUE LIFELONG LEARNING

"The most powerful weapon to conquer the devil is humility. For, as he does not know at all how to employ it, neither does he know how to defend himself from it." —**Saint Vincent de Paul**

"Anti-intellectualism is a sin because it violates Jesus' command to 'love the Lord your God with your mind.'" —**Os Guinness**

"In the last days, when the final exam takes place . . . Love will be the entire syllabus." —**Saint Robert Bellarmine**

The first time I heard someone cuss in church, it was inspirational.

It was the summer before my junior year at Wheaton College. I was back in my old hometown of Hutchinson, Kansas, serving as a youth ministry intern at Crestview Bible Church. The previous semester, I had enrolled in Pulpit Communications, a course on designing and delivering biblical sermons. Now I was eager to put what had I learned into practice: real preaching at a real church.

The kind people at Crestview gave me that chance. At the end of the summer, I was allowed to deliver the message for the Sunday evening service. I was thrilled. Having felt the call to Gospel ministry in general and preaching in particular, I wondered whether—and hoped that—someday I'd be ranked among the great homiletical giants of all time: men like C. H. Spurgeon, P. T. Forsyth, and John R. W. Stott.

I'll probably have to start going by my initials, I thought. *V. R. Kohler!*

The big night arrived. I ascended the pulpit in an olive-green suit, a burgundy and gold flower-patterned tie, and Harry Potter glasses that were uncool before Harry Potter was cool. Even as I looked out at the congregation, I was fantasizing about what I would call the first compilation of my best sermons—the ones that really inspired faith and holiness. I came up with a title for my first octet of messages, connecting my ministry to the Midwest and paying homage to the local collegiate athletic conference: *The Big Eight: The Greatest Sermons of V. R. Kohler, Preacher of the Plains*. Yes, I had great expectations (or, less charitably, earnest delusions of grandeur).

I have always been about three-quarters traditional and conservative and one-quarter maverick and provocateur, so I gave my message a title I thought would raise both interest and eyebrows: "On Being a Passionate Lover." The text was John 12, the account of Mary anointing Jesus's feet with expensive perfume; the main point was that our love for the Savior ought to be costly and extravagant.

It went okay. Or at least that's what I told myself at the time. But the more I thought about it on the way home, the more my satisfaction with my own cleverness started to slide away. Little details of slips or stutters began to sink in. By the time I got back to my room, I was beginning to panic.

If preaching the sermon in real time was disappointing,

listening to it on tape was downright humiliating. I popped the cassette of my message into my Walkman (yes, this was way before MP3s), and my worst suspicions were confirmed: My speech, far from supple and smooth, was pockmarked by "uhs" and "ums." I stumbled over a word at least every couple of sentences, and my voice, far from the rich, resonant baritone I'd hoped for (the kind the Holy Spirit *obviously* prefers to use), sounded more like a prepubescent Boy Scout yelling into a tin can.

And the content wasn't much better. After reviewing my sermon, I concluded that I was, indeed, a master—of clichés, of dull and shopworn ideas, of sloppy exegesis. Worse yet, the only truly dynamic content had (ironically) been pilfered from *Living Above the Level of Mediocrity*—a book by Charles Swindoll, a *real* preacher.

I went to sleep that night deflated and discouraged, daring only to hope that—as Rich Mullins once pointed out—"if God could speak through Balaam's ass, he could speak through me."

The next morning, I felt no better. I drove to the church in a gloomy stupor, bracing myself for the polite but tepid comments that were sure to come. Yet when I walked through the front doors and into the vestibule, I was immediately greeted by Bud, the church custodian. He was beaming.

For most of his life, Bud had been an auctioneer at rodeos all across Kansas—Ft. Scott, Cedar Vale, and Pretty Prairie. In his later years, he helped clean the church. He had the tanned, oaken build of a Kansas farmer, a square jaw, salt-and-pepper hair, and eyes that smiled as much as his mouth. He was the kind of man whose tombstone might be inscribed with the words, "Beef: It's What's for Dinner."

"Oh me oh my," he said to me, reaching out to shake my hand. "You got it, brother!"

"What do you mean?" I asked him.

"You got the gift! You've got a golden tongue," he said. "I was sure blessed by your sermon, brother Vaughn. Mightily blessed."

I was shocked.

"Really?" I said. "Bud, you're just being nice."

That was genuinely what I thought. People there had been incredibly—almost inappropriately—gracious to me. I thought I could have hurled excrement from the pulpit and they'd cheer.

"No, I'm telling you straight," Bud replied. "That was a great message. Blessed my heart."

Bud's unexpected praise stirred my emotions, which I have always worn on both sleeves. I had to work to compose myself. "Well, I appreciate that, Bud. I really do. But to be honest, I felt like I did a terrible job. I feel like a total failure."

"Good," he said.

I was still recovering from the *first* unexpected thing he'd said to me, so this one really threw me for a loop. "Good?"

"Yes. *Good!*" he said. He put his arm around me and leaned forward, as if to whisper some deep knowledge from ancient times.

"Listen, brother: That's *exactly* how you ought to feel. That's exactly *how God wants you to feel.*"

He continued, "If you walk up to that pulpit thinking

that you're God's gift to the congregation, or that you know so much and have everything figured out, what would that tell me about you? It would tell me you're so full of yourself there's no room for Jesus," he said. "Then what good would you be?"

He stuck out his finger and poked me in the sternum. "You'd be good for nothing.

"You'd be nothing more than *a smartass behind the pulpit.*"

Gah! I choked on my surprise and shock and delight. Bud had just cursed in a conservative, quasi-fundamentalist church—and it felt like a blessing.

With fewer words than the Gettysburg Address and no Churchillian eloquence, that spiritual pep talk with a dash of profanity accomplished a great deal. It enlightened and encouraged me. It set me straight and lifted me up. And, to this day, it might be *one of the best sermons I've ever heard.*

Because it got to the heart of the matter: the minute we think we know it all, we know nothing.

That's not to say, mind you, that we cannot have certainty regarding the truth of our faith. It doesn't mean that we can't be confident in the existence of God, the reliability of the Scriptures, or the objective truth of the Resurrection.

What it does mean is that we always need to temper our confidence and conviction with a healthy dose of humility. It means that we recognize that while God's will is perfect, our interpretation of his will is not. We could believe that he wants us to pursue a particular path or make a certain decision—and we could be wrong.

It also means that while God's Word is infallible, our

understanding of it is not. There were many, many Christians (of all traditions) over the course of the centuries who felt very passionately about a particular issue or cause—and as time marched on and the Church gained greater understanding on the issue, it showed that those men and women were in error. (Certain leaders in the Church passionately defended a geocentric view of the universe against Copernicus's "heretical" idea that the earth revolves around the sun, and look how that turned out.)

This is why all of us, no matter how strongly we feel about a particular issue or cause, need to be guided by a deep sense of humility. We need to be open to information and points of view that challenge us. We need to be willing to accept correction and to revise our positions on important matters whether they directly apply to our spiritual lives or not—no matter how long we have held those positions.

In other words, we can never come to the point where we feel we have become infallible masters of the truth. In the Bible, men and women who follow Jesus are called his "disciples." It is significant that the Greek word μαθητής, which we translate in English as "disciple," literally means "learner." A Christian should consider themselves—at heart—a *lifelong learner*.

Ultimately, the main course of study is Jesus Christ himself! We are called to learn everything about the one who refers to himself as "the Way, the Truth, and the Life"—so that we can become more like him, grow closer to him, and transform the world for him.

But beyond that, we are called to recognize, as my alma

mater used to tell its students, that "all truth is God's truth." Another way of putting this is the old maxim, "Everything in the Bible is true, but not everything true is in the Bible." As learners, we are to seek to know and understand truth in every area of life—whether that's in biology or business, mathematics or marketing, finances or philosophy. If something is true, it comes from the one true God himself—and helps us understand him and the world he made far better.

That is why people who want to pursue their God-given potential don't just study the Bible. They study everything! They seek to gain as much knowledge as possible, about every area of life. Not for the purpose of simply stockpiling knowledge so they can feel superior and impress others—instead, the truth they gain *is meant to make them wise*, to help them to fulfill the two greatest commandments: to love God and to love their neighbor (Matthew 22:36–40).

If you are committed to being a lifelong learner, I have four suggestions to help guide you in your humble pursuit of truth:

• **Read often**—and think of books as acquaintances, friends, and lovers. We all have many acquaintances that we know and enjoy on a simple, straightforward level. In the same way, read widely so that you are well acquainted with a variety of subjects and perspectives. However, as you read widely, choose those books that you will take as "friends." I'm talking about the ones that really speak to you, that provide value to you, so that you want to know them fairly well and return to them often. Finally, identify three to five "lovers"—books that you become "intimate" with. Choose titles that you read again and again, spend long periods of time with, reflect upon deeply, and allow to shape your heart, mind, and soul.

• **Take time to write out your thoughts.** The renowned journalist William Zinsser once said, "Writing is thinking on paper." Essayist Joan Didion asked, "How will I know what I think until I write it down?" It's not good to always be reading and never really be thinking about what you've read. Keep a notebook. You don't have to produce genius-level entries. Just scribble down your thoughts. Jot down your ideas. The process of writing helps you organize and clarify the information all tangled up in your head. You don't have to be an actual professional "writer" for this to be helpful. I'm not a professional athlete, but I benefit from going to the gym three times a week! I believe the more you do this, the more you'll love it. There are truths that don't really impact and move us until we take the time to quietly, methodically reflect on them. Once they do, they change our lives. Writing is a practical way to make this happen.

• **Don't let your desire to stay "informed" and be "relevant" lead you to succumb to information overload and distraction.** I think a lot of well-meaning believers try to keep up on news and current events so that they can be better equipped to influence the culture and impact the world. That's an admirable desire. However, keep in mind that in their day, spiritual giants like C. S. Lewis and Thomas Merton did not own a radio or television or read the daily paper on a regular basis, and yet their works remain relevant and influential many years after their deaths! The major media outlets have conditioned us to think that everything is important and urgent. But the truth is, very, very little that happens in the average twenty-four-hour news cycle is significant to our lives. We would all do well to ignore the flood of useless information that comes gushing through our devices on a second-by-second basis, and instead focus on gaining a deeper understanding of the truths and principles that make for a life that is true, good, and beautiful.

• **Remember that "even a broken clock is right twice a day."** That's a saying I have lived by for many years. It means that people who are wrong on one thing can be right on another, and that often people with whom you disagree can provide insight that is true and helpful. So, as someone who wants to be a lifelong learner and seek the truth wherever it may be found, don't discount the thoughts and ideas of those who are very different from you, disagree with you, or are even considered your "enemy." Jesus called us to "love our enemies" (Matthew 5:44). Sometimes, this will mean listening to and learning from them. You might discover that *they are not wrong*—and are not your enemies after all.

Don't forget these four principles. They will guide you as you pursue a life of learning, and seek to become the person God meant you to be.

No matter how wise you become, there will always be more insight you can gain about God and his world. And no matter how good you become—at anything—there will always be room for improvement!

The moment you think you're too good to improve . . .

. . . is the moment you're good for nothing!

QUESTIONS FOR REFLECTION

• One of the signs of humility in a Christian is to be honest about our doubts. Do you ever struggle with believing that God exists, that the Bible is actually God's Word, or that Jesus actually rose from the dead? God is not threatened by your unbelief. Take time to confront your doubts and to work through whatever questions you have. Once you do, your faith will be stronger!

• Have you been a good steward of the mind that God gave you? Do you invest time in learning—whether it's deepening your knowledge of Scripture or growing in your understanding of history or literature—or do you waste all your time playing mindless games, watching worthless movies, or scrolling aimlessly through social media?

RECOMMENDED RESOURCES

• *Humility: The Beauty of Holiness* by Andrew Murray

• *Humility: Wellspring of Virtue* by Dietrich von Hildebrand

• *Love Your God with All Your Mind* by J. P. Moreland

Chapter Sixteen

LET PAIN
EMPOWER YOU

"Suffering produces endurance. Endurance produces character. Character produces hope." **—Romans 5:3-4**

"Christianity teaches that, contra fatalism, suffering is overwhelming; contra Buddhism, suffering is real; contra karma, suffering
is often unfair; but contra secularism, suffering is meaningful. There is a purpose to it, and if faced rightly, it can drive
us like a nail deep into the love of God and into more stability
and spiritual power than you can imagine." **—Timothy Keller**

A s we pursue our God-given potential in this life, why do
we suffer? If our sincere desire is to please God, why do
we have to live with so much pain?

Suffering causes so many people to turn their backs on
God. They just can't wrap their minds around why a good and
all-powerful God would allow people—especially people who
love Him—to experience terrible hurt and hardship.

In the book of Job, the oldest book of the Bible that actually addresses the issue of suffering in the world, God doesn't
ultimately answer Job's question of why so many bad things
happened to him. Instead, he simply asks, "Where were you
when I created the whole universe?" Translation: *I'm God and
you're not. I know things that you don't. Who are you to think you
know better than me?*

135

Ouch! Right?

The reality is, no believer from Job's time to today can really say why God operates the way he does. As Father Cavanaugh said in the movie *Rudy*: "Son, in over thirty years of theological and religious studies, I've come up with two incontrovertible truths: there is a God, and I'm not him!"

But just because we can't know all the reasons God allows suffering doesn't mean we can't understand and embrace *some* of the reasons.

Several years ago, I had an experience that helped me better understand God's motives in allowing and even ordaining that his children suffer. It's a reason that won't fly with the average person. But for those who want to be both strong in faith and mentally tough, it makes total sense.

To help pay my way through seminary in Kentucky, I served as a manager at a family fun park. During my tenure there, I befriended the high school students who worked at the go-kart track, the bumper boat pool, and the miniature golf course. They were great kids, and one summer I decided I would take them on a fun road trip to St. Louis, the city where my folks lived. I thought they'd enjoy the Science Center, the Magic House Children's Museum, and—of course—the Gateway Arch.

For the six-hour trip from Louisville to St. Louis, I decided we needed to drive something other than my increasingly unreliable 1988 Toyota Corolla. So one of the kids asked to borrow the family car, and his dad graciously allowed us to take his brand-new 1998 Lexus GS 300, complete with power moon roof, booming Nakamichi 260-watt audio system, and—most importantly—a three-liter, six-inline engine with double overhead cam and variable valve timing. That engine was a marvel; when it ran, it was soft as a mother's lullaby and smooth as her baby's tummy. But it was definitely a fuel snob—like a connoisseur who insisted on the finest vintage wine, it would only accept premium unleaded gasoline.

Well, about fifteen minutes outside the greater St. Louis metropolitan area, we stopped at a gas station to refuel since we hadn't topped off the tank before we left Louisville. The guys in the back seat hopped out of the car and headed into the convenience store to pick up a snack, and Nikki—my teenage copilot—stepped out of the car to stretch her legs. I opened the gas tank, lifted the nozzle, and started to pump.

Almost immediately, Nikki said to me, "Well, you learn something new every day."

"What?" I asked, standing there with my hands in my pockets as the fuel, surging like a small mountain stream, flowed into the Lexus.

She pointed to the pump. "I never knew that a Lexus runs on diesel."

I froze. I looked at the pump—and my heart jumped into my esophagus. Sure enough: I was pumping diesel into a Lexus GS 300!

"No! No! No!" I cried.

As quickly as possible, I tore the pump from the car. Firing a prayer up to heaven, I ran into the gas station, which (thankfully) doubled as an auto repair shop, spilling my sorry situation to the nearest mechanic.

He stayed calm. "Well, you haven't driven it yet, right?"

No, I told him.

"That's good," he said. "It'll be okay, I think. We're just going to have to siphon that diesel out of the fuel tank."

Siphon? What did that mean?

si·phon [sahy-fuhn]: noun

Definition. 1. a tube or conduit bent into legs of unequal length, for use in drawing a liquid from one container into another on a lower level by placing the shorter leg into the container above and the longer leg into the one below, the liquid being forced up the shorter leg and into the longer one by the pressure of the atmosphere.

Basically, it meant that all the diesel needed to be sucked out of the fuel tank. Correction: it meant that *everything* needed to be sucked out—including whatever premium unleaded fuel was left at the bottom. The fuel tank needed to be completely emptied, and then I needed to pay to fill it up again—from scratch.

In 2 Corinthians 12, Saint Paul writes about his own experience with a siphon. It is not his car's fuel tank that is being emptied, however, but his very soul. "So to keep me from becoming conceited because of the surpassing greatness of the revelations, a thorn was given me in the flesh, a messenger of Satan to harass me . . ." (2 Corinthians 12:7). Biblical scholars have tried to guess what exactly Paul was referring to when he referenced his "thorn in the flesh." Although he personifies it as a "messenger of Satan," some theorize that it was an excruciatingly painful physical ailment. Others think it might have been a person in Paul's life who was a consistent and significant source of opposition and persecution. At the end of the day, we simply don't know. But it doesn't matter. What matters is that whatever the "thorn in the flesh" was, God refused to remove it from Paul's life—in spite of his earnest pleas.

This may make God sound harsh, but he had his reasons—and they were good ones. In 2 Corinthians 12:8–10, Paul writes:

> Three times I pleaded with the Lord about this, that it should leave me. But he said to me, "My grace is sufficient for you, for my power is made perfect in weakness." Therefore, I will boast all the more gladly of my weaknesses, so that the power of Christ may rest upon me. For the sake of Christ, then, I am content with weaknesses, insults, hardships, persecutions, and calamities. For when I am weak, then I am strong.

God's answer to Paul was twofold: first, his grace was sufficient. Second, his power was made perfect in weakness. Essentially, what he told Paul was this: "Paul, I'm not going to remove this difficult source of pain from your life. Why? Because it is emptying you. It is draining you of any tendency toward pride, self-reliance, and independence. And in the absence of these things, it is filling you with something that is far better: my grace." That is why his thorn in the flesh—even though it hurt—was a good thing. It liquidated Paul of himself so that he could be filled with what would—in the long term—be the best thing for him: God!

139

Like that Lexus, Paul may have been filled with the wrong "fuel." The thorn in the flesh was God's siphon to empty him so that he could fill him with something far better: his grace.

I'll be honest: while I was glad the mechanic was able to suck the diesel out of the Lexus, I still thought the whole situation, well, *sucked*. In the end, the car was filled with the right kind of fuel, but my wallet was emptied. It was a tough, expensive lesson for a poor seminary student to learn—and it undercut my enjoyment of that weekend getaway.

Part of me thought, "*Really*, God? You couldn't have steered my hand away from the diesel pump and saved me a week's paycheck? I'm only trying to pay for school *so I can serve you in ministry*! No big deal or anything."

(He might have talked me off the ledge if he would have whispered, *Trust me. You're going to write about this someday in a* New York Times–*bestselling book that will sell over a billion copies!*)

Seriously, though. Nobody enjoys suffering. And there is a level of suffering that people throughout the world experience—including people who very much love Jesus Christ—that we simply cannot fully understand or explain.

We don't have all the answers. But if you don't want to be derailed from your pursuit of your God-given potential, you need to understand why and how God uses suffering. People who go through pain—and you may be one of them—are brought low for a reason. They are emptied of themselves and liquidated of their own self-reliance.

And, as difficult as that may be to experience, it's a very,

very good thing—for "God opposes the proud, but gives grace to the humble." (1 Peter 5:5).

People who are humbled become desperate. They become more motivated—not just to talk a good game, but to act! They go all in on seeking God's help to evolve and improve and to do anything and everything necessary to change their situation for the good.

James 4:10 says, "Humble yourself before the Lord, and he will lift you up."

The reality is, it's very rare for driven overachievers to humble themselves. God uses pain and suffering to lovingly "force" us to do it.

People who successfully move forward toward the fulfillment of their potential—people who have sacred drive!—understand he's not doing it to be a Cosmic Tool.

He's doing it *to lift us up* and make us stronger, more resilient, and better equipped for success. Suffering is good for the soul—and helps us become the kind of people who crush our goals!

QUESTIONS FOR REFLECTION

• Is there a source of pain or suffering in your life? Spend time reflecting on how you might use that "gift of adversity" (as my friend Marcus Aurelius Anderson likes to say) to your advantage? How do you think that God wants to use that "evil" in your life . . . for his glory and the good of the world?

• Pastor Ben Patterson says that people in pain can sometimes become "Cosmic Egotists." In other words, they become so caught up in their own suffering that they forget "the world is bigger than their pain." Are you guilty of this? It's okay to be sorrowful because you're going through tough times. But sorrow is not the same as whining and complaining. These things kill the soul. If you think you are guilty of this, spend time in prayer, asking the Lord to forgive the bitterness of your heart. Ask him if there is anyone who has been negatively affected by your bitter, poor-me attitude, and how you can make things right with them.

RECOMMENDED RESOURCES

• *Walking with God through Pain and Suffering* by Timothy Keller

• *When God Weeps: Why Our Suffering Matters to the* Almighty by Joni Eareckson Tada

• *A Grief Observed* and *The Problem of Pain* by C. S. Lewis

• *The Angel That Troubled the Waters* (*A Short Play*) by Thornton Wilder

Chapter Seventeen

GIVE GOD NOW

"Forget what is behind and strain toward
what is ahead." —**Philippians 3:13**

"There is no tomorrow" —**Apollo Creed**

I s it ever "too late" to pursue our God-given potential? Can we really get "too old" to really start to live?

The average person with the average mindset thinks so. They make a bunch of bad decisions early on in life and think that's torpedoed the rest of their days on Earth. They don't wake up from their zombie existence, where they've done nothing but sleepwalk, until they are forty . . . fifty . . . sixty . . . seventy years old.

At that point, they have a genuine aha moment. They realize that there was so much they could have been and could have done. They are excited for one brief, shining moment, but then they let a lie stop them dead in their tracks.

"It's too late."

Never mind the fact that history is full of people who accomplished amazing things in their twilight years. Never mind the fact that some of the most impactful people of all time did their greatest work right before they died. These people still buy the lie.

They let it keep them from starting to dream, starting to

work, starting to act, starting to achieve, starting to impact . . . starting to live!

People of real faith don't buy that lie. Especially those who have sacred drive.

They know better.

They understand that God can and will do in their lives what he did in the life of one of my good friends' dads.

Years ago, a good friend of mine told me that, for most of his life, his dad was a loser. He neglected his kids. He cheated on his wife. This went on for over twenty-five years.

Then one day something happened—I'm not sure what, but his dad underwent a radical transformation. It was like he woke up from the nightmare of who he was and decided he would do everything in his power to become the man of his family's dreams.

He started reaching out to his kids. He repaired and revitalized his relationships with them, offering himself as a flawed but faithful mentor, friend, and father who wouldn't think twice about taking a bullet for his children.

He sought his wife's forgiveness, did everything he could think of to rebuild trust and reignite love, and pursued her with such happy-go-lucky passion and purpose that he could have inspired a Kenny Chesney country love song.

That lasted one year.

After that, this man learned he had cancer. Terminal cancer.

One year after that, he was gone.

In the space of this man's fifty-something years, for only two did he exist as the best version of himself. For a short

724-day period, he lived and loved in a way that mattered, like he should have all along.

But guess what my friend told me?

"In those two years, he made everything right," he said. "And I kid you not. I am being 100 percent truthful: that's all I remember about him.

"The good years."

No matter how young or old we are, none of us is exempt from the feeling that we have wasted the precious years that God has given us. If you're a little older like I am, you can be tempted to look back over your life and think, "Man, I haven't done anything. And I'm running out of time!"

It's easier for the forty-plus crowd to think that; after all, we're closer to the grave than a college kid or young urban professional (theoretically speaking). But the reality is that none of us, at any age, knows how much time we have left on this planet. You and I could find out tomorrow that we have been stricken with an incurable virus and have forty-seven days to live.

Will it be too late then? For our life to matter?

No.

Because it's not how many days we live but how much of ourselves we pour into our days—or even, if it's all we end up having, one single moment.

Like my friend's dad, we can lose for most of our adult life, but if we end well, we can make a meaningful impact and leave a beautiful legacy behind us.

How is this even possible? It's possible because God is gracious.

One of my favorite poems in the Bible is Psalm 90. In that psalm, Moses muses about how God is eternal but human life is short—just a breath in all of time. All our days "quickly pass and we fly away." In response, he prays, "Establish the work of our hands. Yes—establish the work of our hands."

In other words, he's saying, "Lord, at the end of the day, none of us has long to live. Will you fill us with your grace and goodness and give our lives real weight of impact?"

And that's the thing that the believer with drive knows: God can make one moment "weigh" more than an entire lifetime.

He can make one act of big-hearted generosity or broken-hearted repentance outweigh a lifetime of sins and stupidity.

If you want an example of this in the Bible, look no further than Jesus's conversation with the thief of the cross. Two criminals were crucified with Jesus. One mocked him, but the other said, "Don't you fear God? We are guilty, but this man has done nothing wrong." Then he turned to Jesus and said, "Lord, remember me when you enter your kingdom." And Jesus replied, "Truly, I say to you . . . today you will be with me in Paradise!"

Did you get that? This guy who was being crucified with Jesus had made a hot mess of his life. He was a criminal who deserved death. But in the very act of getting executed, minutes from death, he did one thing that tipped the scales. He entrusted his soul to Jesus, and that changed everything. The weight of the cross he rightly felt on his back was lifted by the work that Jesus was doing on his own cross at that very moment.

His sins were outweighed by God's grace.

So no matter who you are, don't throw away time thinking about years you might have wasted or worrying about how little time you may have left on the planet.

Instead, entrust yourself to the grace and mercy of God, turn your attention to the present moment, and realize, by faith, that what you do RIGHT NOW could have an impact and significance that far outweighs anything that you have said or done up to this point.

Say to God, "Establish the work of my hands. Establish the work of my hands."

Listen . . . At the time I'm writing this, I'm about to have a birthday. I'll be forty-seven years old.

Not gonna lie. Been feeling a little melancholy, a little disappointed.

Not because I haven't accomplished all that I wanted to by this age (although I haven't), but because by this age, I figured I would have matured spiritually and become a far better man than I actually am.

It's humbling.

Oh, I'm not beating myself up.

It just is what it is.

The good thing is, I come from a family where I have learned that (1) you can make up for lost time and (2) you can always finish well.

My maternal grandmother, Emma Lotter, went into a deep depression after my aunt took her own life. Mom-Mom Em was seventy years old when she plunged into despair. It got so bad she barely ate or took care of herself. But ten years later, she came out of it, admitted that she had just been angry at God, and asked the Lord if he would graciously give her some "bonus years" to make up for the time she had wasted.

She lived until she was one hundred years old.

And, yes, she made the most of those bonus years, living and serving others with the joy of Jesus.

It's never too late to make a comeback, folks.

You just have to admit you were wrong to fritter away the precious time God gave you—and ask him to make up for it.

He is willing to do that, if you ask.

The key is that you have trust God to help you make the most of your time . . . and do everything you can to finish well.

My dad was diagnosed with intestinal cancer August 2014. It took him fast. By November 2014, he was gone.

The chemo treatments weakened him considerably. But in spite of that, he kept working as a church organ salesman.

That's a pretty niche industry, you know? Not the easiest product to sell! But man, my dad loved organs; and he worked hard to keep selling them until the day he died, so that there'd be more money coming in for my mom to live on.

A couple months after my dad passed, I was invited out to Phoenix to the annual dealer meeting for Rodgers Organs, the company my dad worked for for over forty years.

During the closing ceremonies, they announced that, in the four months before he died, my dad sold more organs than he had ever sold in his career, during a four-month stretch of time.

When all was said and done, he had sold nearly a half-million-dollars' worth of church organs!

See, my dad didn't use cancer as an excuse to mail it in. *He finished well.* I don't care if you think you don't have a lot of time left.

I don't care if you know you don't have a lot of time left.

You can finish well.

If you want to be a person who really makes an impact on this earth, ask God to fill your life with his grace so that every positive action you perform weighs a ton.

And dedicate the present moment to being thankful for the impact of God's grace in your own life. Then turn around and make an impact on the world . . .

On each person that you meet TODAY . . . Give God now . . .

. . . and start right now!

QUESTIONS FOR REFLECTION

• What are things that, looking back, you realize you haven't paid enough attention to or put enough effort into? How could you still invest yourself into those things while you have time?"

• Do you feel like your days are getting away from you? Do you fear that time is slipping through your fingers and that you're wasting your life? Carve out five to ten minutes a day and commit them to turning your attention to God. Express your fears to him. Ask him to help you make the most of your time on Earth, and "establish the work of your hands."

RECOMMENDED RESOURCES

• Psalm 90 (a psalm of Moses)

- *Crazy Busy: A (Mercifully) Short Book About a (Really) Big Problem* by Kevin DeYoung

CONCLUSION

I zola Curry was a disturbed woman.

She could barely keep a job or stay in one location for more than a couple of months. Her neighbors said she was "antisocial." "Odd." "A little scary." In the late 1950s, she moved to New York and managed to get a job as a housekeeper. At that time, it became clear that this wasn't just a garden-variety "crazy woman." She suffered from serious mental illness. She was paranoid. Delusional.

And the main focus of her paranoia and delusion was the National Association for the Advancement of Colored People.

It might have been understandable for Izola Curry to fear and hate that organization if she were some racist or white supremacist. But the NAACP was dedicated to racial reconciliation.

And Izola Curry was black.

It didn't matter to her, though. She thought the organization was a front for terrorists. She thought everyone in the NAACP was *really* a communist! In her mind, the group was persecuting her. They were after her—they were the reason she couldn't get a job, that her life was miserable.

Though she didn't like any of them, there was one man that she really despised. He was the leader—he was working with the communists, spearheading the attack against her. She wondered: "How can I get him before he gets me?"

She got her chance a couple months later.

The man, a controversial public figure who had just published a book, was at a signing event in nearby Harlem, New York. Curry arrived dressed for a black-tie event—it was an important moment for her, so she wore what witnesses described as "an elegant, stylish suit, jewelry, and sequined cat's-eye glasses."

Dressed to the teeth, she entered the bookstore with a loaded .25-caliber pistol and a long, sharp metal letter opener hidden in her purse.

She pushed her way through the crowd to the table where the man was sitting. As he signed the books, he smiled gently, greeting people and speaking kindly to them. When Izola reached him, she asked who he was. She wanted to make sure.

When he answered, she pulled out the letter opener and stabbed him in the chest.

She almost managed to get *all seven inches* of metal into his chest, and he doubled over, gushing blood. When security grabbed her, she yelled, "I've been after him for six years! I'm glad I done it! I'm glad I done it!"

The man was rushed to the hospital. The situation was bad—it would take careful, delicate surgery to remove the blade without killing him in the process. The operation, which required three of the most dedicated, skilled surgeons, went on for hours. There was little hope that it would be successful.

But thank God for the man . . . and for our country . . . it was.

The man remained hospitalized for weeks after the attack. Several months later, telling the press about the whole story, he revealed a shocking detail of the ordeal: "The razor tip of the instrument had been touching my aorta. So my whole chest had to be opened to extract it. Dr. Maynard . . . one of the surgeons who operated on me, told me, 'If you had *sneezed* during the hours you waited for us to begin the operation . . . your aorta would have been punctured and you would have drowned in your own blood.'"

Think about that.

That man was just a sneeze away from certain death. Just a sneeze away!

Up until that point, he had already made a powerful impact on the country. He was already committed to doing good. As he once said, "The time is always right to do what is right." But you know what?

I think that whole brush with death gave him a deeper sense of how fragile human life really is.

That man already lived with a sense of urgency, but I think that after getting stabbed, that sense of urgency went into overdrive!

Years later, in a great speech the man gave, he said he was glad he hadn't sneezed. If he had, he would have missed out on so many of the amazing things that happened in his life. He wouldn't have witnessed firsthand the great victories that his people achieved over racism and oppression. He wouldn't have been able to participate in so many marches for freedom. He wouldn't have seen how hate was overcome by LOVE.

But you know what? At that end of that speech, this is what the man said to his audience:

Like anybody, I would like to live a long life.
Longevity has its place. But I'm not concerned
about that now. I just want to do God's will.

And he's allowed me to go up to the mountain.

And I've looked over.

And I've seen the promised land.

I may not get there with you. But I want you
to know tonight, that we, as a people, will get to
the promised land!

And so I'm happy tonight.

I'm not worried about anything.

I'm not fearing any man!

Mine eyes have seen the glory of the coming
of the Lord!

When I first read that, I thought, *That's a man who knew he
had lived his life well and was ready to die.*

And on the VERY NEXT DAY after he gave that speech,
that man went to see God.

He died. Actually, he was killed. Shot by an evil man named
James Earl Ray.

The date was April 4, 1968. That was the day the United
States—and the whole world—lost Dr. Martin Luther King Jr.

The speech he delivered the night before he was killed is
called the "I've Been to the Mountaintop" speech. It's a great
one. But it's not his best one. We all know his best one. It
ends with these words:

When we allow freedom to ring, when we let it
ring from every village and every hamlet, from

every state and every city, we will be able to speed up that day when all of God's children, black men and white men, Jews and Gentiles, Protestants and Catholics, will be able to join hands and sing in the words of the old Negro spiritual, "Free at last! free at last! thank God Almighty, we are free at last!"

The impact that Martin Luther King Jr. had on America, and the world, was amazing. He led an extraordinary life, to a very large degree, because he had a real brush with death. That sense of his own mortality drove him to really embrace what he believed.

He carried himself with an air of clarity and authority. He engaged people with intentionality and intensity. He lived with a sense of urgency. Why? How?

Because he knew that someday he was going to die.

The fear of being persecuted for pursuing peace and justice. The fear of being wronged for doing what was right. The fear of being hated for being a person of love. All those fears were overcome by the greater fear that he would come to the end of his earthly life and in his last moment say, "I never really lived the life God meant me to live."

Psalm 144:4 says, "A man's life is like a breath; his days are like a passing shadow."

Hebrews 9:27 says, "It is appointed for everyone once to die; and after that, the Judgment."

Ephesians 5:16 says, "Make the best use of your time, because the days are evil."

In the latter verse's context, that phrase means, "the days are desperate." There are crazy things going on. That was true back then. It's true today. But the craziness of the world is not a reason for fear. It is a reason for a sense of urgency. It is a reason for action. It is a reason to live with all your might, while you yet live.

What is the key to becoming truly exceptional—to making the most of your life?

It is the recognition that someday—maybe someday soon—you are going to die!

For this reason, don't be afraid to go all in on life—to go all in on who you were meant to be. But as you go all in and fearlessly embrace your passions, make sure those passions are driven not just by a desire for your own gain, but for the good of the world and the glory of God. As John Piper said, "Whatever you do, find the God-centered, Christ-exalting, Bible-saturated passion of your life, and find your way to say it and live for it and die for it. And you will make a difference that lasts. You will not waste your life."

Don't fear any pushback you get from the world. Push yourself beyond your comfort zone. As Pope Benedict XVI said, "You are not called to a life of comfort, but a life of greatness." You can only achieve greatness if you're fearless enough to pursue it. And paradoxically, you can only possess that kind of fearlessness if you live with a healthy fear of God—the recognition that someday, perhaps someday soon, you are going to die and stand before your Maker.

When you die, you're going to stand before Jesus. By God's grace, you're going to be able to say, "While I lived, I lived with all my might. I accepted the forgiveness you offered on the cross, I trusted in your mercy and goodness, and I made the most of my life. I wasn't a coward. I lived with faith. And I lived fearlessly!"

And after you say that, you'll hear the words that will eradicate all fear from your heart, not only in that moment, but for all eternity. You'll hear Jesus say, "Well done, good and faithful servant! Enter now into the joy of your master!"

Even after those with a strong *sacred drive* have overcome their indiscipline, their vices, their softness, and their insecurity, fear can be the hardest thing to conquer. We worry—quite understandably—about physical danger, risky decisions, and our ability to stand against a challenging world. And all that's nothing compared to the knowledge that one day, we're going to die. The good news is, you don't have to crush those fears. All you have to do is acknowledge them, understand them, and recognize that something greater than them is with you every single moment—God's purpose for your life.

I certainly haven't crushed my fears. That is to say, I haven't found a way to chase them off forever. Like you, I am regularly assaulted by the fears that are common to everyone on this planet: the fear of other people's opinions. The fear that we'll be rejected for being ourselves. The fear that we'll be marginalized because of something we believe or some way we choose to live. The fear that our vices will get the better of us. The fear that we will be overcome, not by any external opposition, but by our own internal demons. The fear of suffering. The fear of failure.

The battle with fear is a universal human experience. No wonder the command "do not be afraid" (or some variation of that phrase) is found more often in the Bible than any other command. Apparently, we are people who have a natural inclination for fear. That's the bad news.

The good news is that God has revealed to us truths about himself and his universe that can help us overcome our fears and experience freedom. Truths about his motivating grace, his use of suffering to strengthen us, and his ability to use one moment of time to transform our lives. I'm talking about the truths in this book I've tried to explain and apply to your life, to the best of my ability. These are the truth I've used to motivate myself, every day, to pursue my God-given potential. These are the truths I've tried to embrace and internalize, in order to help me cultivate my own sacred drive and continue to pursue my God-given potential . . .

. . . for my own gain . . .

. . . the good of the world . . .

. . . and the glory of God!

Any fear you and I have in life should be overcome by the greater fear of not really living the life God meant us to live. For those with sacred drive, when the choice is giving in to fear or going after that purpose, it's no contest.

That's how we can be free—free at last!—to pursue our God-given potential and make the most of our lives!

ABOUT THE AUTHOR

Vaughn Kohler is a writer, speaker, spiritual director, and consultant who currently serves as director of development for St. Isidore's Catholic Student Center in Manhattan, Kansas. From 2015–2019, he served as cohost for *The MFCEO Project*, one of the top-rated business and success podcasts in the world. In addition, he has been a magazine editor, ghostwriter, content marketer, and adjunct instructor for undergraduate and graduate-level communications courses. A former evangelical pastor, Vaughn joined the Catholic Church in 2011. He and his wife, Kasia, live in Manhattan with their four daughters. Find him online at vaughnkohler.com.

HOW DO WE MAKE THE MOST OF OUR LIVES? HOW DO WE PURSUE HAPPINESS AND SUCCESS IN A WAY THAT IS TRUE, GOOD, AND BEAUTIFUL?

To book speaking engagements or one-on-one sessions, or to subscribe to Vaughn's *Sunday Best Weekly Newsletter* visit www.vaughnkohler.com.

Made in the USA
Coppell, TX
08 April 2021